The Game

A Comedy in Three Acts

By Harold Brighouse

SERVING THEATRE

S F

SINCE 1830

WWW.SAMUELFRENCH.CO.UK
WWW.SAMUELFRENCH.COM

FOR AMATEUR PRODUCTION ENQUIRIES

UNITED KINGDOM AND WORLD EXCLUDING NORTH AMERICA

plays@SamuelFrench-London.co.uk

020 7255 4302/01

Each title is subject to availability from Samuel French, depending upon country of performance.

PREFACE

In another age than ours play-books were a favourite, if not the only, form of light reading, and the novel, now almost universally preferred, is the development of the last century. But a writer of plays should be the last person in the world to resent the novelist's victory, for plays are written to be acted, and reach a full completeness only by means of the collaboration of author with producer, scene-painter, actors and, finally and essentially, audience. The author's script bears to the completed play a relationship similar to that of an architect's plan to a completed building.

Architect's plans, however, are not unintelligible to the layman, especially to the layman who is not devoid of imagination, the layman who is ready to spend a trifling mental effort and to become, be it ever so little, expert. And so with printed plays, those ground-plans of the drama. There must have been in the eighteenth century, a larger percentage of the reading public than obtains to-day that was expert in reading plays; plays were thought—you can find ample proof of it in the Diarists—easier reading than the novels of Fielding, Richardson and Smollett. Perhaps the comparative brevity of a play was, even in those unhurried days, a point in its favour; certainly the play-reading habit was strong and one likes to think that it is not lost. To read dully the script of a spectacular play is desolating weariness, but the same script read with sympathetic imagination becomes the key to fairyland, and from an armchair one sees more marvels than ever stagecraft could present. There are abominable limitations on the stage; producers are tedious pedants; but the reader mentally producing a play from the book in his hand looks through a magic casement at what he gloriously will instead of through a proscenium arch at the handiwork of a merely human producer. Play-reading, in fact, obeys the law that as a man sows so shall he reap; a little trouble, rapidly eased by practice, leads one to a great deal of pleasure.

It depends, of course, upon the play as well as upon the reader, and though one has rather romantically instanced spectacular plays, their scripts do, as a rule, belong to the class of play which is not worth reading. They are, or are apt to become, the libretto to some specific scenery or stage effect and the imaginative reader, failing to hit upon the particular staging intended, is lost in puzzlement. Nor do plays of action make the best reading. There are no plays but plays of action, but action is of many kinds, and the play whose first concern is situation and rapid physical movement is so specifically a stage-play, so sketchy in its ground-plan until the collaborators work in unison upon it, as to make reading more of a torment than a pleasure. While you must have wordless pantomime at the basis of every play, it is those plays which exhibit in high degree the use of action in the form of dialogue that are the more comfortable reading; and, always postulating that a play is a play—not necessarily a playwright's play, the admiration of hit brother craftsmen, but a thins practicable, actable and effective on the stage—the more physical action is subordinated to character, to the exploration of the springs of human motive, the better it is for reading purposes and the better for all purposes.

Ibsen led the modern play, where the modern novel followed it, to the investigation of character rather than to the unfolding of a story, and one suggests that readers who find satisfaction in the modern psychological novel should find the reading of modern plays to their taste for the reason that the dramatists, though they haven't in a play the same opportunities for analysis as the novelists find in their more spacious pages, are essentially "out for" the same thing.

The type of play one is here writing about is one which has not, in the past, flourished extensively in the popular theatres; it is the type known, rather obscurely, as the "Repertory" play. It was called by that name, probably in derision, and the Repertory play was held to be synonymous with the un-commercial play. Then queer things happened. "Hindle Wakes" broke out of the Repertory palisade, made dramatic history and, what from the amazed commercial manager's standpoint was even more startling, a fortune; "The Younger Generation" followed into the commercial camp; and in the rent profiteer's year of 1919, when managers seemed forced by ruthless circumstance more even than by inclination to play the safest game and to offer the Big Public nothing but repetitions of .the tried and true, two plays from the Repertories came to town. "The Lost Leader" filled the Court Theatre in a very heat wave, and "Abraham Lincoln" took the King to Hammersmith—with many thousands of his subjects. So that it will not do to speak of plays as commercial on the one hand and Repertory on the other. Repertory has golden possibilities, if you don't expect too much of it. It would be fallacious to expect the same pay-dust from "Abraham Lincoln" as from "Chu Chin Chow." Nor would one expect Joseph Conrad to sell like Nat Gould.

Sincerity is a virtue possessed, as a rule, by the Repertory play, but it will by no means do to claim for this sort of play a monopoly of sincerity. The most popular type of drama (and the most English), melodrama, is rigidly sincere—to the confounding of the Intellectual. There is plenty of dishonest thinking and unscrupulous play-making, but not in popular melodrama. In melodrama which pretends to be something other than what it is, there is immediate and obvious insincerity, but there is no writing with the tongue in the cheek in downright, unabashed melodramas of the old Adelphi, and the present Lyceum type. It will not do to call the "highbrow" plays sincere, with the implication that all other plays are insincere, any more than they can themselves be sweepingly characterized as uncommercial. Sincerity, anyhow, may be beside the point, and the term Repertory play, though unsatisfactory, stands for something perfectly well understood. No definition would be apt to the whole body of Repertory plays, but one would like, diffidently, to suggest that Repertory plays are written by men and women of intellectual honesty who postulate that their audience will be composed of educated people—and that attempt at a definition fails. It has a snobbish ring.

And now, after generalizing about Repertory plays and reading plays, to come down to the particular instance of the Lancashire plays here printed. They are three of seven plays which their author has written about the people of his native county, and reasons for publishing them now are that nobody wanted to publish plays during the war, and that the author is an optimist about the future of Repertory. Which last is only a sort reason for publishing some of Repertory's step-children— that, at any rate, the new men may know, if they care to know, these workaday examples deriving from the only Repertory Theatre in Great Britain which created a local drama. Though none of these three plays was, in fact, produced by Miss Horniman's Company, they nevertheless belong to the "Manchester School," which was a by-product of her Company.

The "Manchester School" was never conscious of itself, as the Irish School was. The Irishmen had a country, a patriotic sentiment, a national mythology; they had, so soon after the beginning that it seemed they had it from the first, the already classical tradition of Synge; they had in the Deidre legend a subject made to their hands, a subject which it appeared every Irishman must tackle in order to pass with honours as an Irish dramatist; and there was explicit endeavour to create an Irish Drama. In Manchester, so far were we from any explicit ambition to create a Lancashire Drama that we denied the fact of its creation. What reputation it had was not home-made in Manchester and exported, but made in London and America. At Miss Horniman's theatre in Manchester, there were so many bigger things being done than the earlier, technically weak plays of the local authors. And it is worth pointing out that the authors went (it was admirable, it was almost original in them) for their material to what was immediately under their nose; they took as models the Lancashire people of their daily life, and in their plays they did not always flatter their models. The models saw themselves in the theatre rather as they were than as they liked to think they were, and they hadn't the quixotry to praise too highly authors who held up to them a mirror of disconcerting truthfulness. It came upon the authors unexpectedly, as even something a little preposterous, to be taken seriously, to be labelled, heaven knows by whom, the "Manchester School," as if they had a common aim.

That, surely, is the significance of the "Manchester School," that the phenomenon and the hope. Miss Horniman established her Company in Manchester, with Mr. B. Iden Payne, a genius, as her producer of plays. What she gave to Manchester was perhaps more, perhaps not more, than the aftermath of the historic Vedrenne-Barker campaign at the Court Theatre; at any rate, she gave a series of Repertory plays—plays which had no likelihood of being seen in the provinces under the touring system—notably well acted; she demonstrated that drama was a living art, and in the light of that demonstration there outcropped spontaneously, un-self-consciously, the body of local drama now known as the "Manchester School." Whatever the individual merits of the Lancashire plays may be, whatever, even, their collective importance or unimportance, they have this significance of localization. Stimulated by Miss Horniman's catholic repertoire, local authors sought to express in drama local characteristics.

There are no two questions in the writer's mind, nor, he thinks, in anybody's, as to whether local drama is or is not a good thing. It is more than ever good in to-day's special London conditions, but it was always good in and for its own locality, and very good when it broke away from home, travelled to London and introduced to Londoners authentic representations of natives of their country. It brought variety where variety was needed. Not all the plays of the "Manchester School," of course, have travelled. One or two, indeed, hardly travelled across the Gaiety Theatre footlights, and in the case of a few others, mostly one-act plays, there was never the least chance of their emerging from Lancashire owing to the fact that they were written deliberately in dialect. A most racy little piece, "Complaints," by Mr. Ernest Hutchinson, with its scene laid in the office of an Oldham spinning-mill, is a case in point. One doubts, even, if the comparatively urbane Manchester audience grasped the whole of its idiomatic dialogue. But these are the extremes of local drama, and generally, the Lancashire writers have avoided dialect as, in the first place, impracticable, and in the second place, disused, except (to quote Houghton) "amongst the roughest class in the most out-of-the way districts." Accent is not dialect though possibly originates in it. Even when one wishes to use dialect one must not, for stage purposes, write it as it is spoken. The dramatist selects his material from dialect as he selects his larger material from life. Dramatically correct dialect is literally incorrect; it is highly selected dialogue which indicates, but does not obscure, and the true dialect dramatist is not the man who exactly imitates the speech of a district, but he who most skillfully adapts its rhythms and picks out its salient words. Synge invented an Irish dialect which is false in detail and infinitely true in broad effect, and the "Manchester School," faced with the same difficulty, has solved' it in the same way, hoping, though without much confidence, that the Lancashire cadences it adopted and used in its very few dialect plays may sound to alien ears as aptly as the language of Synge's Irish sounds to our own. Though you may search in vain the dialogue of Mr. Allan Monkhouse's plays for local characteristics, the "Manchester School" has as a rule indicated by the use, in greater or less degree, of local idioms that the speech of Lancashire has a well-marked individuality; but dialect, as a distinctive variant of the national language, can hardly be said to exist in Lancashire.

One labours the point a little in order to make clear that the "Manchester School" had no dental advantage, over writers who lived near other provincial Repertory Theatres, in the existence of a language whose dramatic literature they felt urged to create; there was no such language. And its absence makes a curiosity of the fact that from Manchester alone of the Repertory centres has any considerable body of local drama emerged. (Dublin is another matter; one speaks here of Great Britain.) Other Repertory centres, like Birmingham and Bristol, must have local characteristics: Liverpool is, geographically at any rate, in Lancashire; and Glasgow has a language of its own. None of these Repertories was sterile, but even Birmingham, despite Mr. John Drinkwater and "Abraham Lincoln," was economical in creativeness and fathered no local drama. Must the conclusion be that the Manchester atmosphere has, with its soot, a vitalizing dramatic principle?

Possibly; but a less fantastic theory is that Manchester had Miss Horniman, and other Repertories had not. Again one insists that the Lancashire plays were a by-product, and a by-product only, of Miss Horniman's Company. Who in their senses would go to Manchester expecting to evoke a local drama? And if she had gone there with a prejudice in favour of poetic plays, it is more than likely that no local drama would have been evoked. Modern Lancashire is industrial Lancashire—one forgets the large agricultural oases, while nobody but map-makers and administrators remembers that a slice of the Lake District is in Lancashire—and industrialism does not inspire the poetic play. Miss Horniman began, on the contrary, with a season whose best productions, though it included Maeterlinck, were Shaw's "Widower's Houses" and McEvoy's "David Ballard." Those two productions seemed, rightly or wrongly, to fix the type of play preferred by Miss Horniman's Company; it happened—let us call it realistic comedy—to be the type by which the life of Lancashire could be best expressed in drama and the future authors of the "Manchester School," most of them of an impressionable age, some of them already fumbling their way to dramatic expression, seized avidly the type and the opportunity. They were not so provincial as to have to wait for Miss Horniman to come to be introduced to Shaw: but there are worlds of difference between reading Shaw, even between seeing him indifferently produced, and a Shaw play transmuted by the handling of such a producer as Iden Payne. It is putting the case without hyperbole to say that Miss Horniman's Company was an inspiration.

The Repertory whose "note" is the poetic play will probably evoke no local drama, because, until we get the village Repertory, local drama is the drama of the modern town, wherein the stuff of poetry exists, if at all, only as a forced revival of folk-lore. Anything can be great poetry to the great poet; one speaks here of the average playwright, the observer of his fellow man in a provincial town, seeking his medium of expression in drama; and such a man is unlikely to find it in the poetic play or to find encouragement and inspiration from a Repertory where poetic plays are visibly preferred. It is almost to be said that Miss Horniman's Company and the Birmingham Repertory Theatre stand for rival theories of the drama, but not quite; they have too much, including Shakespeare, in common.

Local drama is too important to be left so specially in the hands of Miss Horniman and the "Manchester School." It is important for the localities and important, too, for London; London is quite as ready to be interested in good plays about people in Aberdeen or Halifax as in plays about people in New York, but the New York author lives in a city where plays are produced and the Aberdeen author does not. The stimulation of local drama is possible only where a local producing theatre exists; the education of a dramatist unfinished until he has heard his lines spoken and watched his puppets move. Drama in the capitals is standardized to some half-dozen patterns which alter slowly and, failing the local producing theatre, what is the provincial author to do but to suppress his originality and to write plays, in hopes of London production, as near as he can make them to one of the approved current designs? It is said that were it not for the continued influx from the provinces, London would die out in three—or is it two? —generations; and if that is true of life, it is true also of drama, and the plain duty of those who control British Drama, the Napoleons of the theatre, is to dig channels whereby healthy provincial blood may flow to London to revitalize its Drama.

This, which means that Sir Alfred Butt ought to seek out a number of intelligent producers and endow them in provincial Repertory theatres to work without interference from above, but always with the vigilant eye for that by product of a rightly inspired Repertory, local drama, is a simple matter of commercial self-interest, on a par with the action of the magnates of scientific trade who endow research not out of love of science, but in the expectation that they will be able some day to exploit profitably the resulting discoveries. So might Sir Alfred Butt exploit local authors discovered by the producers of his far-flung Repertories. The theatre is either a business or a gamble, and in the hands of men like Sir Alfred Butt it looks less like a gamble every day. Enlightened business self-interest would look a little to the future, to the fostering of authorship in provincial towns, to the establishment of many Repertories.

To come back to the windfalls of the "Manchester School" printed here. They fell, one of them in the Gaiety Theatre, Manchester, at a time when Miss Horniman's Company was on vacation; another at the Liverpool Repertory Theatre, which was in origin a secession from Manchester headed by the late Miss Darragh, with the plays produced by Mr. Basil Dean, later the first Liverpool Director; and the third so far away from Manchester as the Empire Theatre, Syracuse, New York State, linked with Manchester, for all that, through being produced by Mr. Iden Payne. In reading them again, one is startled for the thousandth time by the difference between stage and study. The third act of "The Northeners" makes curious reading, because it depends partly upon the juxtaposition of the characters on the stage, partly upon the suggestion "off" of a ruse plagiarized from the Punic Wars, partly upon a spectacular "curtain," but it is production proved it—in the focus of the theatre. It "came off" on the stage. Laughter in theatre is, again, a mystery. It is possible that the Lancashire plays in general have the characteristic of acting more amusingly than they read. "Hindle Wakes" reads positively austerely; acted, it is full of humour; and one's recollections of "The Game" on the stage make for the same conclusion. It has, in the theatre, a far more pronounced tendency to set its audience laughing than seems apparent in its text. In the case of "Zack" the fun is, one would say, hardly of a subtle kind. Taking the "Manchester School," bye and large, and remembering the charge against it that it was "grey" or "dreary," one is forced to believe either that Lancashire humour is not everybody's humour— Mrs. Metherell in "The Game" might almost be set as a test—or else that the "Manchester School" has been confused with the whole body of Miss Horniman's productions; and, even if so, the charge fails.

There was an Icelandic tragedy produced in the early days of her Company, which depressed the thermometer alarmingly; there was Verhaeren's "The Cloister," a great play performed to empty houses, adding insult to injury by being popularly called "dreary," and the chill resulting from those two productions, one a mistake of management, the other a mistake of the public, lasted for years. The case of the Lancashire Plays is clear; their authors aimed at presenting the human comedy of Lancashire, and if their dramatic purpose was to be achieved by the alternative uses of laughter or of tears, they preferred to achieve it by the ruthless light of laughter. Many of the plays have not been printed and the appended bibliography includes no examples of the comedy of Mr. H. M. Richardson, Dr. F. E. Wynne or Mr. M. A. Arabian. Incomplete record of the Lancashire Plays as it is, it serves to drive home the contention that the "Manchester School" are, in the main, comic writers.

Bibliography: (1) Stanley Houghton— "The Works of Stanley Houghton," three volumes (Constable & Co.); "Hindle Wake!" (Sidgwick and Jackson); "The Younger Generation," "Five Short Plays," "Independent Means," "The Dear Departed," "Fancy Free" (Samuel French, Ltd.). (2) Allan Monkhouse—"Mary Broome," "The Education of Mr. Surrage" (Sidgwick & Jackson); "Four Tragedies" (Duckworth & Co); "War Plays" (Constable & Co.). (3) Harold Brighouse— "Hobson's Choice," "Garside's Career' (Constable & Co.); "Dealing in Futures," "Graft" (Samuel French, Ltd.); "Lonesome-Like," "The Price of Coal," "Converts," (Gowans & Grey, Ltd). (4) Judge E. A. Parry— "The Tallyman and other Plays" (Sherratt & Hughes). (5) J. Sackville Martin— "Cupid and the Styx" (Samuel French, Ltd.).

CHARACTERS

AUSTIN WHITWORTH

EDMUND WHITWORTH

LEO WHITWORTH

JACK METHERELL

HUGH MARTIN

DR. WELLS

BARNES

ELSIE WHITWORTH

FLORENCE WHITWORTH

MRS. METHERELL

MRS. WILMOT

MRS. NORBURY

The Action of the Play takes place in a Lancashire town on the last Saturday in April between the hours of one and five in the afternoon.

ACT ONE

AUSTIN WHITWORTH's *house in Blackton was built by his father in 1870 and the library is a stately room. The door is on the right. Centre is a deep bay with a mullioned window and padded window seat. A brisk fire burns in the elaborate fireplace, with its high club fender. Shelves line the walls. All the furniture dates from the original period of the house, and though the chairs may have been upholstered in the meantime, they would repay fresh attention. Solidity is the keynote of the room, but its light wood and bright rugs save it from heaviness.*

The time is one o'clock on the last Saturday in April. A painting of old John Whitworth is over the fireplace.

In the armchair is EDMUND WHITWORTH, *a prosperous London solicitor. A bachelor, his habit of dining well has marked his waist-line. Pompous geniality is his manner. In his hand is a sheet of notepaper which, as the curtain rises, he finishes reading. Sitting facing him on the fender is* LEO WHITWORTH, *his nephew.* LEO *is twenty-one and dresses with fastidious taste, beautifully and unobtrusively. He is small. Just now he awaits* EDMUND's *verdict with anxiety.* EDMUND *removes his pince-nez and hands the paper to* LEO.

EDMUND I like it, Leo.

LEO Really, uncle? I asked you to be candid.

EDMUND Yes. I do like it. It's immature, but it's the real thing. *(Rising and patting his shoulder patronizingly)* There's stuff in you, my boy.

LEO You're the first Whitworth who's ever praised my work. The usual thing's to laugh at me for trying to be a poet.

EDMUND A prophet in his own country, eh? Perhaps they don't know very much about poetry, Leo.

LEO (*excitedly, walking about, while* EDMUND *takes his place by the fire*) Is that any reason for laughing at me? I don't know anything about hockey, but I don't laugh at Flo and Elsie for playing. As I tell them, mutual tolerance is the only basis for family life. If I were a large-limbed athlete they'd bow down and worship, but as I've got a sense of beauty and no brawn they simply bully the life out of me.

EDMUND You're sure you do tolerate them?

LEO Of course I do. I'd rather have a sister who's a football maniac any day than a sister who's a politician. There's some beauty in catching balls, but there's no beauty in catching votes. What I complain of is that there's no seriousness in this house about the things that matter.

EDMUND Such as—poetry?

LEO Oh, now *you're* getting at me. All right. I'm used to it. Being serious about poetry's better than being serious about football, anyhow.

EDMUND Sonnets have their place in the scheme of things.

LEO A high place, too.

EDMUND I agree with you in putting them above football.

LEO Then you'll find yourself unpopular here.

EDMUND At the same time, it's possible to overdo the sonnets, Leo.

LEO Never. Art demands all.

EDMUND My dear boy, if you're going to talk about art and temperament, and all the other catchwords—

LEO I'm not. I'm only asking you to tell them you believe in my genius and then they'll drop thinking I'm making an ass of myself.

EDMUND I see. By the way, what are you making of yourself, Leo?

LEO A poet, I hope.

EDMUND I meant for a living.

LEO I have a weak lung.

EDMUND Is that your occupation?

LEO It is my tragedy.

EDMUND Um.

LEO You will speak to them for me, uncle? They'll listen to you. At least you come from London, where people are civilized.

EDMUND Are they? In London I hold a brief for the culture of the provinces.

LEO You took jolly good care to get away from the provinces, yourself. And you mustn't tell me you think Blackton is cultured.

EDMUND I heard my first Max Reger sonata in Blackton long before London had found him.

LEO Music's another matter.

EDMUND Yes. Your father played it to me.

LEO Well, there you are again. Music and football are the only things he cares about. That's just what I complain of. I've tried to raise his tastes, but I find generally a lack of seriousness in men of his age. Of course' there are exceptions.

EDMUND Thank you.

Enter **FLORENCE WHITWORTH,** *in golfing tweeds with bag, and without hat, hair tumbled by the wind. She is a large-made girl of eighteen, supremely healthy and athletic.*

FLORENCE May I hide in here?

LEO What's there to hide from?

FLORENCE Eleanor Smith is tackling Elsie in the hall to play hockey for the High School Old Girls this afternoon. When she finds Elsie won't, she'll want to try me, so I'll keep out of the way, please.

EDMUND And why won't Elsie?

FLORENCE We never do when the Rovers are playing at home. I wouldn't miss seeing the match this afternoon for the best game of hockey I ever had. *(Slinging the golf-bag in a corner)* Topping round on the links, uncle. You ought to have come.

EDMUND I'm a sedentary animal, Flo.

FLORENCE Yes. And you're putting on weight. It's six years since you were here, and I'll bet you've gone up a stone a year.

EDMUND In my profession a portly figure is an asset. If you have a lean and hungry look, clients think it's because you sit up late running up bills of costs. If you look comfortable, they imagine you're too busy dining to think of the six and eightpences.

FLORENCE Yes. I never met a slacker yet who wasn't full of excellent excuses. Leo calls his poetry. You call yours business. Wait till you'll retire. You'll find it out then if you haven't a decent hobby.

EDMUND But I have.

FLORENCE It's invisible to the naked eye. You don't golf, and you don't play tennis or cricket or—

EDMUND I collect postage stamps.

FLORENCE No wonder you're in bad condition with a secret vice like that. *(Goes to open window)*

LEO *(sharply)* Don't do that.

FLORENCE It's blazing hot. I can't imagine what you want a fire for.

LEO Uncle felt chilly.

FLORENCE Sorry I spoke. No, I'm not. It serves him right for taking no exercise.

Enter **ELSIE WHITWORTH**, *who, like* **FLORENCE**, *is tall and muscular, but with a slim beauty which, contrasted with* **FLORENCE**'s *loose limbs and occasional gawkishness, is, at twenty-two, comparatively mature. Her indoor dress, to honour the visiting uncle, is elaborate and bright.*

ELSIE Flo, Eleanor Smith wants you.

FLORENCE I know she does. That's why I'm hiding in here.

ELSIE They're a man short on the team, and—

FLORENCE Didn't you tell her I can't play to-day?

ELSIE She thinks she can persuade you.

FLORENCE She can't.

ELSIE You'd better go and tell her so.

FLORENCE (*gathering up her golf-bag*) Blow Eleanor Smith! She thinks hockey's everything. I hate fanatics.

ELSIE She's waiting for you.

FLORENCE All right. I'll go. (*Exit* **FLORENCE**)

ELSIE Heard the news, Leo?

LEO Not particularly.

ELSIE (*excitedly*) Jack Metherell's coming in to see father before the match. Father told me.

LEO Oh? My pulse remains normal.

ELSIE You've no more blood in you than a cauliflower. I'm tingling all over at the thought of being under the same roof with Metherell?

EDMUND May I enquire who Mr. Metherell is?

ELSIE Do you mean to say you've never heard of Metherell?

EDMUND I apologise for being a Londoner.

ELSIE That's no excuse. They can raise a decent crowd at Chelsea nowadays.

EDMUND Indeed? I live at Sevenoaks.

ELSIE You must have heard of Metherell.

EDMUND No. Who is he?

LEO Metherell is a professional footballer, uncle.

EDMUND Oh!

ELSIE (*indignantly*) A professional footballer! He's the finest centre forward in England.

EDMUND (*politely*) Really? Quite a great man.

LEO Quite. He's the idol of my sisters and the Blackton roughs. For two hours every Saturday and Bank Holiday through eight months of the year forty thousand pairs of eyes are glued on Metherell and the newspapers of Saturday night, Sunday and Monday chronicle his exploits in about two columns; but if you don't know what "agitating the spheroid towards the sticks" means, you'd better not try to read them.

ELSIE *approaches him threateningly.*

He is also good looking and a decent fellow.

ELSIE You'd better add that.

LEO I will add more. He spends the rest of his time training for those two hours, and when he's thirty he'll retire and keep a pub; and in three years eighteen stone of solid flesh will bury the glory that was Metherell.

ELSIE *(threatening him)* You viperous little skunk.

LEO I appeal to you, uncle. Can a skunk possess the attributes of a viper?

ELSIE If you say another word against Jack Metherell, I'll knock you into the middle of next week. You're frightened of the sight of a football yourself and you dare to libel a man who—

LEO The greater the truth the greater the libel. You're a solicitor, uncle. Isn't that so?

EDMUND Do you want my professional opinion?

LEO *(dodging round the table from* **ELSIE***)* I want your personal protection.

ELSIE *(giving* **LEO** *up)* Uncle, Jack Metherell's the truest sportsman who ever stepped on to a football field. He's the straightest shooter and the trickiest dribbler in the game. I'd walk barefooted over thorns to watch him play, and for Leo to say he'll retire at thirty and grow fat is nothing but a spiteful idiotic lie.

EDMUND *(making peace)* Well, suppose we say he'll retire at thirty-five and just put on a little flesh and live to a ripe old age, fighting his battles over again.

LEO Over a gallon of beer in the saloon bar.

ELSIE If your head wasn't too full of poetry for anything important, you'd know Jack's a teetotaller. He's never entered a public house and he never will.

EDMUND If I were you, Leo, I wouldn't quarrel. I should make a poem about it.

ELSIE It's all he's fit for. Lampooning a great man. I tell you, uncle, Jack Metherell can do what he likes in Blackton. If he cared to put up for Parliament, no other man would make a show.

LEO Oh, the fellow's popular. They all love Jack.

ELSIE Popular. There isn't a woman in the town but would sell her soul to marry him.

EDMUND This seems to be the old Pagan worship of the body.

LEO The mob must have a hero. Prize-fighting's illegal and cricket's slow, so it's the footballer's turn to-day to be an idol.

ELSIE Look here, you can judge for yourself this afternoon.

LEO Are you coming to the match, uncle?

EDMUND Yes. I'm curious to see it. I suppose you're not going?

LEO Oh, I shall go.

EDMUND Really? I had gathered that you don't like football.

LEO I don't like funerals or weddings either, but they're all the sort of family function one goes to as a duty.

ELSIE A duty. Will you believe me, he never misses a match, uncle?

LEO If you want to know, I go for professional reasons.

EDMUND Professional?

LEO I am training myself to be a close observer of my fellow men, and in a football crowd I can study human passions in the raw. To the earnest student of psychology the interest is enormous.

ELSIE Yes. You wait for his psychological shout when Blackton score a goal. You'll know then if his lungs are weak. We go because we like it and so does he, only we're not ashamed of our tastes and he is. Wait till Jack Metherell comes on the field this afternoon in the old red and gold of the Blackton Rovers and—

AUSTIN WHITWORTH *enters while she speaks and interrupts her. Without being grossly fat,* **AUSTIN** *is better covered than* **EDMUND**, *whose elder brother he is. Without exaggeration, his lounge suit suggests sporting tendencies. His manner is less confident than that of* **EDMUND**, *the successful carver-out of a career, and at times curiously deferential to his brother. Obviously a nice fellow and, not so obviously, in some difficulty. With his children he is on friendly chaffing terms, so habitually getting the worst of the chaff that he is in danger of becoming a nonentity in his own house. He wears a moustache, which, like his remaining hair, is grey.* **FLORENCE** *follows him.*

AUSTIN But Metherell won't.

ELSIE What. Has Jack hurt himself at practice?

AUSTIN No.

LEO What's up with him?

AUSTIN Nothing.

ELSIE Then why isn't he playing?

AUSTIN He is playing.

ELSIE You just said—

AUSTIN He won't wear the Blackton colours. He's playing for Birchester. He's transferred.

ELSIE You've transferred Jack Metherell! Father, you're joking.

AUSTIN No.

ELSIE *(tensely)* I'll never forgive you. He's the only man on the team who's Blackton born and bred. The rest are all foreigners.

FLORENCE Who've you got to put in his place? There isn't another centre forward amongst them.

AUSTIN There's Angus.

FLORENCE Angus! He can't sprint for toffee, and his shooting's the limit.

AUSTIN Well, you've to make the best you can of Angus. Metherell belongs to Birchester now.

ELSIE I don't know what you're thinking about, father. Are you mad? What did you do it for?

AUSTIN Money, my dear, which the Club needs badly.

ELSIE It'll need it worse if we lose to-day and drop to the second division.

AUSTIN We must not lose to-day.

FLORENCE You're asking for it. Transferring Metherell. The rest are a pack of rotters.

AUSTIN They've got to fight for their lives to-day. Birchester offered a record fee on condition I fixed at once. I was there last night with Metherell and he signed on for them.

FLORENCE It's a howling shame.

LEO And over Blackton Rovers was written Ichabod, their glory is departed.

ELSIE Father, do you mind if I go? I might say some of the things I'm thinking if I stayed.

FLORENCE I'll come too. I wish to goodness I was playing hockey. It won't be fun to see Jack Metherell play against us.

FLORENCE *at door.*

AUSTIN It wasn't for fun that I transferred him.

ELSIE No. Worse. For money. You've told us that and—oh, I'd better go.

Exeunt FLO *and* ELSIE.

AUSTIN Go with them, Leo.

LEO Shall I?

AUSTIN Please.

Exit LEO.

Well, Edmund?

EDMUND *(puzzled)* Well, Austin?

AUSTIN Now you can judge exactly how pressing my necessities are. You've heard it all.

EDMUND Really? You've only talked football.

AUSTIN Football is all. I'm sorry I got in last night too late to have a chat with you, but *(shuddering)* what I was doing yesterday is public property this morning.

EDMUND You mean about the man Metherell?

AUSTIN Yes.

EDMUND I understand some other club has bought him from you. Are footballers for sale?

AUSTIN Er—in a sense.

EDMUND And why have you sold him if he's a valuable man?

AUSTIN He's invaluable. If ever there was a one-man team, that team is ours. I've seen the others stand around and watch Metherell win matches by himself. But to-day money is more essential than the man.

EDMUND I'm still puzzled. Is football a business then?

AUSTIN Of course. That's the worst of burying yourself in London. You never know anything. Football clubs to-day are limited companies.

EDMUND I fancy I had heard that.

AUSTIN Well, broadly speaking, and not so broadly either, I am the limited company that runs Blackton Rovers. You never cared for sport. I was always keen. In the old amateur days, I played for Blackton while you went country walks and studied law. Football's always meant a lot to me. It means life or death to-day.

EDMUND That's a strong way of talking about a game, Austin.

AUSTIN Life or death, Edmund. Blackton's been my passion. It's not a town that's full of rich men, and the others buttoned up their pockets. Employers of labour too, who know as well as I do that football is an antidote to strikes, besides keeping the men in better condition by giving them somewhere to go instead of pubs. I've poured money out like water, but the spring's run dry and other Clubs are richer. They can buy better players. They bought them from me.

EDMUND Have the men no choice?

AUSTIN Up to a point. But footballers aren't sentimentalists and rats desert a sinking ship. The one man who stuck to me was Metherell. He's a Blackton lad, and he liked to play for his native town. To-day, he's gone. I made him go for the money I needed. The Club's been losing matches. We were knocked out of the Cup Tie in the first round. Lose to-day and Blackton Rovers go down to the second division. My Club in the second division!

EDMUND Does that matter so much—apart from sentimental reasons?

AUSTIN It matters this much. That there'll never be another dividend. The gate money for the second division game's no use to me.

EDMUND But surely, if your public's got the football habit they'll go on coming.

AUSTIN Not to a second division team. They'll drink a pint or two less during the week and travel on Saturdays to the nearest first division match.

EDMUND So much for their loyalty.

AUSTIN They don't want loyalty. They want first class football, and if I can't give it them, they'll go where they can get it. As it is, the Club's on the brink of bankruptcy, and I'm the Club.

EDMUND Then your men had better win to-day.

AUSTIN They must.

EDMUND And if—supposing they don't?

AUSTIN That's why I brought you here. To look into things. I can't face ruin myself.

EDMUND Ruin? It's as bad as that?

AUSTIN Oh, I daresay you're thinking me a fool.

EDMUND I think your sense of proportion went astray.

AUSTIN All my money's in it. I don't care for myself. I had value for it all the day four years ago when Blackton won the Cup at the Crystal Palace, but it's been a steady decline ever since. What troubles me is, it's so rough on the children.

EDMUND Have you told them?

AUSTIN What's the use? Leo's got no head for business and the girls are—girls.

EDMUND Yes. Tell me, what are you doing with Leo?

AUSTIN Doing? Well, Leo's is a decorative personality, and he has a lung, poor lad. Leo's not made for wear.

EDMUND Rubbish! If he's made you feel that, he's a clever scamp, with a taste for laziness and a gift for deception.

AUSTIN Well, I do feel about Leo like a barndoor fowl that has hatched out a peacock.

EDMUND Peacock! Yes, for vanity. A little work would do the feathers no harm.

AUSTIN I can't be hard on a boy with his trouble.

EDMUND I foresee a full week-end, Austin. And I thought I was coming down for a quiet time in the bosom of my family.

AUSTIN Yes, we've been great family men, Edmund, you and I.

EDMUND *(hastily)* Well, we won't go into that again.

AUSTIN Yes, we will. We quarrelled over Debussy. Come into the music-room and I'll play the thing over to you now. If you don't admit it's great, I'll—

EDMUND We've other matters to discuss, Austin. This isn't the time for music.

AUSTIN Yes, it is. Music makes me forget. Some men take to drink. I go to the piano.

Enter **FLORENCE** *and* **ELSIE**.

ELSIE Father, do you want any lunch?

AUSTIN *(looking at watch)* By Jove, yes. Time's getting on. I'll play that Debussy thing afterwards, Edmund. Coming, girls?

ELSIE No, thank you, father. Neither Flo nor I feel we can sit down to table with you just yet. We've had ours.

AUSTIN You've been quick about it. Where's Leo?

FLORENCE Stuffing himself with cold beef. Men have no feelings.

EDMUND Surely Leo must have a feeling of hunger.

ELSIE It's indecent to be hungry after hearing of father's treachery to Blackton.

AUSTIN Treachery!

FLORENCE Some of my tears fell in the salad bowl, and I hope they'll poison you.

EDMUND Be careful what you're saying, Florence. Is that the way to talk to your father?

FLORENCE No. That's nothing to the way I ought to talk to him.

EDMUND Well, I know if I'd addressed my father like that—

FLORENCE It's a long time since you had a father to address, Uncle Edmund. We bring our fathers up differently to-day.

EDMUND If you only knew what your father—

AUSTIN *(taking his arm)* It doesn't matter, Edmund. Come to lunch.

Exeunt EDMUND *and* AUSTIN.

FLORENCE Yes, it doesn't matter if the Rovers are defeated, but there's beef and beer in the next room and the heavens would fall if food were neglected.

ELSIE Oh, I don't care if they are beaten. The Rovers don't interest me without Metherell.

FLORENCE I don't believe they ever did. You're no true sportswoman, Elsie. You always thought more about the man than the game. You might be in love with Metherell.

ELSIE Yes, I might.

FLORENCE Perhaps you are.

ELSIE Is there a woman in Blackton who doesn't admire him?

FLORENCE Oh, I admire him. But that's not loving.

ELSIE No. That isn't loving.

FLORENCE You sound jolly serious about it.

ELSIE Do you realize that now he's transferred he'll have to live in Birchester—two hundred miles away?

FLORENCE Yes, I suppose so.

ELSIE What are our chances of seeing him?

FLORENCE Once a year or so when Birchester play here, instead of about every alternate Saturday.

ELSIE I've been seeing him oftener than that.

FLORENCE Do you mean you've been meeting him?

ELSIE *(breaking down on* **FLO**'*s shoulder, to her great embarrassment)* Flo, I do love him and I don't care who knows it, and now he'll have to leave Blackton, and I—

FLORENCE Steady, old girl. I'm a bit out of my depth myself, but I'll do my best for you with father.

ELSIE *(braced up)* Father wouldn't stop me.

FLORENCE He might try. Jack isn't quite our class, in a general way of speaking, is he?

ELSIE Class! What is our class? We're nobodies.

FLORENCE Still, as things go in Blackton we're rather upper crust, wouldn't you say?

ELSIE Grandfather began life as a mechanic's labourer.

FLORENCE Did he? I've never worried about our pedigree, but you wouldn't think it to look at him. *(Looking at his portrait)*

ELSIE Oh, he made money. One of the good old grinding, saving sort. But he began a good deal lower down than Jack. Jack's father was an undertaker.

FLORENCE An undertaker!

ELSIE *(hotly)* Well, I suppose undertakers can have children like other people.

FLORENCE Oh, I've no objections

ELSIE I've no objections either.

FLORENCE I daresay not—to the father. He's dead. But the mother isn't.

ELSIE What's the matter with his mother?

FLORENCE Haven't you seen her?

ELSIE Jack's shirked introducing me, if you want to know.

FLORENCE Well, I *have* seen her, and—

ELSIE Well?

FLORENCE She's a hard nut to crack.

ELSIE I'll crack her if she needs it. If I want to marry a man, I marry him. I don't mind telling parents about it, but I don't ask their permission. That sort of thing went out about the time motor cars came in.

FLORENCE Then why haven't you told father before this?

ELSIE Because Jack's old-fashioned and thinks he ought to speak to father first. He's got a perfectly ridiculous respect for father.

FLORENCE Father's his employer. *We* don't think much of father, but I expect there *are* people who regard him as quite a big man.

ELSIE That needn't have made Jack a coward. As father's ceased to employ him perhaps he'll get his out-of-date interview over now. *(She runs suddenly to window)*

FLORENCE What's the matter?

ELSIE I'm sure I heard a ring.

FLORENCE You've got sharp ears. Do you mean to tell me that in this room you can hear a bell in the kitchen?

ELSIE *(opening window)* It might be Jack.

FLORENCE *(following her)* Don't you know whether it is?

ELSIE I can't see any one.

FLORENCE But I thought people in your case didn't need to see. Don't you feel his unseen presence in your bones like you feel a thunderstorm?

They are both in the window bay. **BARNES**, *the butler, shows in* **JACK METHERELL**. **JACK** *is dark and handsome with traces of coarseness, tall and of strong appearance, clean-shaven, dressed rather cheaply but not vulgarly. A modest fellow, unspoiled by popular acclaim and simple-minded though successful. He remains near the door, not seeing the girls.* **FLORENCE** *restrains* **ELSIE**.

BARNES I will let Mr. Whitworth know you are here.

JACK Thank you.

BARNES *half closes door, then returns.*

BARNES Mr. Metherell, I was thinking of having a little money on the team this afternoon. Can I take it from you that it's safe?

JACK It depends which team you put it on.

BARNES Why, the Rovers, of course.

JACK Do you want to win your bet?

BARNES I do that.

JACK Then put it on Birchester.

BARNES Really, Mr. Metherell?

JACK Really.

BARNES *pauses, then.*

BARNES I will inform Mr. Whitworth that you are here.

Exit **BARNES**. **JACK** *watches him close door, then goes to bookcase, examines books, takes one out and begins to read studiously.* **FLORENCE** *motions* **ELSIE** *to remain and comes forward.*

FLORENCE Good-morning, Mr. Metherell.

JACK *(closing book quietly)* Good morning, Miss Florence.

FLORENCE Are you much of a reader?

JACK I'm striving to improve my mind.

FLORENCE *(taking the book)* Good gracious, you've got hold of Plato.

JACK Yes. I have read him in the *Everyman* Edition, but I see this is a different translation by a Mr. Jowett.

FLORENCE How learned you must be.

JACK Not I, more's the pity. We've two members in the Mutual Improvement League at our Sunday School who can read Plato in the original. I wish I could.

FLORENCE Do you? I'll put it back. *(Replacing book)* You'll have no use for Plato in a minute.

JACK Why not, Miss Florence?

> FLORENCE *laughs and exit, leaving him looking after her.*
> ELSIE *comes forward and puts her hands over his eyes.*

It's Elsie.

ELSIE Yes. It's Elsie. *(Facing him)* Aren't you going to kiss me, Jack?

JACK In your father's house?

ELSIE It's as good as any other place.

JACK No, it isn't. Not till I have asked his leave.

ELSIE You've kissed me in the fields.

JACK I know. I've compromised with my conscience.

ELSIE Jack, if the rest of you was as antiquated as your conscience, you'd be a doddering octogenarian instead of the liveliest player in the League. Have you come now to ask father's leave?

JACK I've come because he told me to last night. I might ask his leave though, now. But I think I ought to ask my mother first.

ELSIE They'd better both be told at once. If you're going to Birchester, I'm coming with you.

JACK You've heard that then?

ELSIE Yes. Did you hear what I said?

JACK About coming with me?

ELSIE Yes.

JACK I'm willing if they are.

ELSIE Who are "they"?

JACK Your father, and my mother. Suppose the banns go up next Sunday, we could get married in a month and make one bite of the wedding and the testimonial do they'll want to give me.

ELSIE I couldn't be ready in a month, Jack.

JACK Well, I'm ready any time.

She kisses him.

Oh, now Elsie, that's a foul. You know—

ELSIE You didn't kiss me. I kissed you. I do what I like in this house.

JACK It's a big house, lass. You'll find less breathing space in my seven-and-six a week house in a row, with my mother in it, and all.

ELSIE *(pulling him to the arm-chair and sitting herself on its arm)* I've thought it all out, Jack. It won't be a house in a row. There are moors round Birchester, and we're going to live outside the town in a dinky little cottage where the air will always keep you at the top of your form, and I shall have a garden to look after and be handy for the links. I'm going to teach you golf. I shall drop hockey when I'm married. Married life demands sacrifices.

JACK Yes. You're going to sacrifice a lot.

ELSIE You're not going to begin all that over again, are you? Do you want to marry me?

JACK Like nothing on earth.

ELSIE Then I get you and nothing that I lose counts against that gain.

JACK You've a fine sweet way of putting things. I just go funny-like all over and the words won't come. But I love you, lass, I love you. I'll be a good husband to you.

ELSIE It's heaven to hear you say you love me. I want no sweeter words to come than those, I don't deserve it, Jack. Who am I? Elsie Whitworth. Nothing. And you're the grandest, strongest player of your time.

JACK *(rising)* You think too much of football, Elsie.

ELSIE That's impossible.

JACK You do. Football's as good a way as another of earning a week's wages, but that's all it is.

ELSIE It's the thing you do supremely well.

JACK Yes. Now and for a few more years maybe, but I'll be an old man for football soon.

ELSIE That's why I mean to teach you golf. Don't I tell you I have thought about it, Jack? You're going to be as brilliant at golf as now you are at football. I'll never lose my pride in you, your huge, hard muscles and your clean fit body.

JACK It's a great thing to be strong and master of your strength.

ELSIE Your splendid strength! Your swiftness and your grace.

JACK But it's a greater to be clever, and I'd give up all my strength if I could write a poem like the one your brother wrote in the *Blackton Evening Times.*

ELSIE *(contemptuously)* Leo! That weakling.

JACK He may be, but he's got a brain.

ELSIE You're twenty times the cleverer.

JACK Then I'm good for something better than football. I'm up in football now as high as I can get. I used to dream of being called the finest player in the League. They've called me that these last two seasons and my dream's grown bigger. I'm honoured for my play. I'd like to gain some honour now for work.

ELSIE You've just told me football *is* work.

JACK I mean brain work. A footballer's a labouring man. And I want you, Elsie. I look to you to lead me to the higher path.

ELSIE *(dejectedly)* You think I can!

JACK I know you can. You've got a fancy now for football, but it's not your real self. You're a cultured woman.

ELSIE *(interrupting)* Culture doesn't count.

JACK *(proceeding)* You've gone beyond the things that puzzle me. You're at the other side. Why, Elsie, there are things in Browning that I can't make out, and Walter Pater has me beat to atoms.

ELSIE Those aren't the real things, Jack.

JACK They're real enough to be the things that made me want you. I could pick and choose from lots of women fit to talk of football to me, but I'm tired of football. You're the only woman who can talk to me of other things—and you won't.

ELSIE You're tired of football!

JACK Not of the game. Sick of the eternal jaw about it.

ELSIE Well, I'm sick of books.

JACK You can't be that. Books last.

ELSIE Your fame will last. Books aren't the real thing.

JACK Then what is real?

ELSIE Blood. Flesh and blood. I'd burn every book in this room for the glory of another rush like yours when you scored your second goal last Saturday. It may have lasted thirty seconds, but it was worth a wilderness of books.

JACK It was worth just half a column in the *Athletic News*.

ELSIE It's worth my love for you. It's not your brain I'm wanting, Jack. It's you. You're splendid as you are. Don't try to hide behind a dreary cloud of culture. It's better fun to be alive all over than to crawl through life with a half-dead body and a half-baked mind.

JACK Life's not all fun.

ELSIE It isn't, but it ought to be, and for you and me it's going to be, and if you don't stop looking serious, I'll upset you by kissing you again.

JACK Don't do that, Elsie. It isn't right yet.

ELSIE Jack, you've a bilious conscience. It's the only part of you that isn't gloriously fit.

JACK Give me till I've seen your father and then perhaps you'll tire of being kissed a long while sooner than I tire of kissing you.

ELSIE It's so stupid to ask father about a thing like that. It's not his lips you're going to kiss. It's mine.

JACK I've to satisfy my conscience, Elsie.

ELSIE The poor thing needs a lot of nourishment.

Enter AUSTIN *and* EDMUND.

Don't stint it.

AUSTIN Good morning, Metherell. Elsie, we've to talk business.

ELSIE Mayn't I stay? Men are so funny when they're serious.

AUSTIN *(holding door)* You would find no entertainment this time.

ELSIE *(passing him)* That's all you know about it.

Exit ELSIE.

AUSTIN Sit down, Metherell. Oh, this is my brother, Mr. Edmund Whitworth.

EDMUND *(shaking)* I'm pleased to make your acquaintance, Mr. Metherell.

They sit down, AUSTIN *commanding the room from the club-fender.*

AUSTIN Very busy that train we came home by last night, Metherell.

JACK Yes, very full.

AUSTIN I couldn't get a chance of talking to you. Now, it's about this match to-day.

JACK Yes?

AUSTIN You know how tremendously important it is for Blackton.

JACK Blackton 'ull be a second division team next season.

AUSTIN I hope not, Metherell.

JACK (*without arrogance*) With me playing against them?

AUSTIN I still hope not. Blackton must not lose today.

JACK I don't see how they can help it.

EDMUND You've a good opinion of yourself, I notice, Mr. Metherell.

JACK Blackton Rovers without me aren't a team at all. They're certain to be beaten.

AUSTIN You say that as if you don't mind if they are.

JACK I belong to Birchester now, Mr. Whitworth.

AUSTIN Come, Metherell, you've belonged to Birchester for half a day. You belonged to Blackton for five years. This match can make no difference to Birchester. They're half way up the list. It's critical for Blackton. You've played all these years for Blackton and you've thought Blackton all your life. You can't change your allegiance all in a moment. You can't pretend you'd like to see Blackton go down.

JACK Oh, I've a fondness for Blackton. I don't deny it.

AUSTIN Metherell, Blackton must win to-day.

JACK They might have done if you hadn't transferred me.

AUSTIN My hand was forced.

JACK So you told me.

AUSTIN At heart you're still a Blackton man, Metherell.

JACK Maybe. But at Football I've signed on to play with Birchester. I may be just as sorry as yourself to see Blackton go down to-day, but as centre forward of Birchester United it's my bounden duty to do my best to send the Rovers down.

AUSTIN Look here, Metherell, you see the hole I'm in. What am I to do?

JACK I've no suggestions.

AUSTIN What about the referee?

JACK Eh?

AUSTIN Anything to be done there?

JACK I don't understand.

AUSTIN Could I square him?

JACK Not unless you want to see him lynched.

AUSTIN Then you're the only hope.

JACK It's a poor hope if you're looking for anything of that from me.

AUSTIN I'm asking you to be loyal to Blackton for another day.

JACK Were you loyal when you transferred me?

AUSTIN Yes: loyal to Blackton's very existence. Don't play your best this afternoon. That's all I ask.

JACK I always play my best.

EDMUND Are you never out of form, Mr. Metherell?

JACK I play at the top of whatever form I'm in.

EDMUND Couldn't you make it convenient to be in particularly bad form to-day? After your long journey to and from Birchester yesterday, a tired feeling's only natural.

JACK I'm feeling very fit. Do you know you're asking me to sell a match?

AUSTIN (*firmly*) Yes.

JACK I couldn't square it with my conscience. I really couldn't, Mr. Whitworth. I know it means a lot to you, but I'm not that sort, and you ought to know it.

AUSTIN Your conscience might be—salved.

JACK Salved?

EDMUND Yes. Just let us know how much you consider will cover
all moral and intellectual damages, will you?

JACK *(to* AUSTIN*)* I'm glad it wasn't you who spoke that word.

AUSTIN I endorse it, Metherell. I told you last night how I stood.
The loss of to-day's match may involve my ruin.

JACK As bad as that? I'm sorry.

AUSTIN Man, can't you see I'm not romancing? Do you think
I'd come to you with this if I wasn't desperate?

JACK It's a pretty desperate thing to do. Suppose I blabbed?

AUSTIN Yes. There's that. It ought to show you just how desperate
I am. You know, and no one better, how this Club's been
run. You know there's blackguardism in the game, but
Blackton hasn't stooped. Whatever other clubs have done,
Blackton has stood for sport, the straight, the honest game.
The Blackton Club's my life's work, Metherell. I might have
done a nobler thing, but there it is, I chose the Club. I gave
it life and kept it living, and the time's come now when
I can't keep it living any more. Twice top of the League and
once winners of the Cup. It's had a great past, Metherell, an
honourable past. It's earned the right to live, and now it's
in your hands to kill the Blackton Club and end the thing
I've fostered till it's seemed I only lived for that one thing.
It isn't much to ask. A little compromise to save the Club
you've played for all these years, to save the club and me.

JACK I cannot do it, Mr. Whitworth.

AUSTIN *sinks hopelessly into armchair.*

EDMUND *(briskly)* Now you referred to your conscience,
Mr. Metherell. My experience is that when a man does
that he's open to negotiation.

JACK Money won't buy my conscience, sir.

EDMUND *(half mockingly)* Well, are you open to barter?

JACK No. The thing I want from you is no more to be bought
than my conscience is.

AUSTIN *(without hope)* You do want something from me, then?

JACK I want to marry Elsie.

EDMUND *(shocked)* My God!

AUSTIN Does she know? *(Rising)*

JACK Does she know? She says we're to be married and that's all about it, but I'm old-fashioned and I want your leave.

EDMUND My niece and a professional footballer!

AUSTIN Steady, Edmund. Now, Metherell, just let us see where we stand. You propose to help Birchester to beat Blackton.

JACK I'll do my best.

AUSTIN And you think I'll let you ruin me first and marry my daughter afterwards?

JACK I won't buy Elsie from you at the price of my professional honour.

AUSTIN Professional fiddlesticks! The thing's done every day.

JACK Not by a Blackton lad. I've learnt the game you taught me, Mr. Whitworth, the straight, clean Blackton game. I'll not forget my school even at the bidding of the head. I'm not anxious to be suspended for dishonest play.

AUSTIN Only incompetents get suspended. You needn't fear. You're skilful.

JACK Not at roguery.

EDMUND You're talking straight, Mr. Metherell.

JACK Yes. It's you that's talking crooked.

Enter **ELSIE.**

ELSIE May I come in now?

AUSTIN No. We're busy.

ELSIE Thank you. *(Closing door)* You don't get rid of me twice with that dear old business bogey. I expect Jack's made an awful mess of it. Has he told you about us, father?

AUSTIN No. Yes. Go away. We're talking seriously.

ELSIE Yes. You all look very foolish. Is it settled, Jack?

JACK No.

ELSIE What's the trouble? Is father being ridiculous?

EDMUND Upon my word, Elsie—

ELSIE Oh, that's all right, uncle Ed. It does father no end of good to be talked to like that. Jack, I find I can be ready in a month after all, so that's all right.

EDMUND Ready for what, girl?

ELSIE My wedding, uncle. You'd better start thinking about your present.

AUSTIN But—

ELSIE Hasn't Jack told you we're to be married?

AUSTIN He's told me he wants to marry you, but—

ELSIE Then what is there to argue about? Men do love making a fuss about nothing and fancying themselves important. Come along, Jack. You're going to take me down to the ground.

EDMUND Well, I'm—

ELSIE Oh, dear no, Uncle. You're not.

> **ELSIE** *goes off with* **JACK**. *They reach door.*

Curtain

ACT TWO

The office of Blackton Football Club is situated under a stand, the slope of which forms its roof, down to some eight feet from its floor. In the perpendicular side are the windows, overlooking the ground. Used as much for the entertainment of visitors as for office work, the room contains only a desk with revolving chair, and a sofa to indicate its titular purpose, and for the rest is a comfortably appointed club-room. On the walls are sporting prints and, by the desk, a file of posters, the uppermost advertising the day's match. A door gives access, and a second door leads to the ambulance-room.

HUGH MARTIN, *the Club Secretary, sits at the open desk.* **AUSTIN** *enters.*

AUSTIN Well, Martin.

MARTIN Good afternoon, Mr. Whitworth.

AUSTIN What do you estimate the gate at? Five hundred pounds?

MARTIN *(rising)* The returns are not in yet, but hardly that much.

AUSTIN *(looking out of window)* I should call it a twenty thousand crowd by the looks of it.

MARTIN *(not looking out)* Not far short. But *(awkwardly)* there's been a little accident, sir.

AUSTIN Accident?

MARTIN Oh, it's happened before. They rushed the turnstiles on the shilling side.

AUSTIN I say, Martin, that's too bad. Just when we need every penny we can screw.

MARTIN About three thousand got in free before the police could master the rush.

27

AUSTIN That Chief Constable's an incompetent ass. He never sends us enough men.

MARTIN Fewer than usual to-day. There's a socialist demonstration on the recreation ground, and that's taken away a lot of police.

AUSTIN Idiot! Does he think Blackton people will go to a political meeting when there's a football match?

MARTIN As you say, sir, he's a fool.

AUSTIN *(sitting at desk)* No use claiming for the loss either. Pass me the cheque-book, Martin. Those people with the mortgage on the stands threaten to foreclose unless we pay on Monday. I'd a letter this morning.

MARTIN *(opening safe and passing cheque-book from it)* Can we meet it, sir?

AUSTIN Yes. Metherell's transfer fee is in the Bank.

MARTIN That brightens our sky.

AUSTIN Think so, Martin?

> **MARTIN** *replaces* **AUSTIN** *at desk, signs cheque, tears it out and then puts book back in safe.*

MARTIN I never thought we should live through the season. And here we are at the end of it still alive and kicking.

AUSTIN They'd better kick to some purpose to-day, Martin, or—

MARTIN It'll be all right, sir.

AUSTIN You're a sanguine fellow. Suppose we lose. Second Division. No dividends. No dividends, no Club. No Club, no Secretary, Martin.

MARTIN Don't talk about it, sir. It's not losing my job. That doesn't matter. But the thought of Blackton going down is more than I can bear.

AUSTIN Yes. It's ugly. You're a good fellow, Martin.

MARTIN Don't mention it, sir. I love the game.

AUSTIN The game! Yes. Always the game.

MARTIN I often wish this side didn't exist, though it is my bread and butter... That's the whistle. They're playing.

AUSTIN Yes. Didn't you know? They'd begun before I came in here.

MARTIN (*reproachfully*) Oh, sir!

AUSTIN Don't let me keep you from your place.

MARTIN Aren't you coming?

AUSTIN No. I shan't see much of this match, Martin.

MARTIN When so much depends upon it!

AUSTIN Yes. That's why.

MARTIN (*consolingly*) But you forget things when you watch the game.

AUSTIN (*kindly*) Go and forget them, Martin.

> *Enter* **FLORENCE**, *in outdoor spring costume, excitedly.*

FLORENCE Father, aren't you coming? You've missed it all. We've scored a goal in the first five minutes.

AUSTIN Scored already! Thank God.

FLORENCE The most glorious goal you ever saw. Blackton are playing up like little heroes. It's the match of the season.

> **MARTIN** *slips out.*

Angus is in terrific form. I take back what I said about him. Metherell himself couldn't do better. He had the Birchester goalee beat to smithereens. I tell you it's tremendous.

AUSTIN How's Metherell playing?

FLORENCE Against us.

AUSTIN (*impatiently*) Yes. But how?

FLORENCE How does he generally play?

AUSTIN Like that? He's in form?

FLORENCE It's worth a guinea a minute to watch him. And you're missing it.

AUSTIN I'll go on missing it, Flo.

FLORENCE *(looking through window)* Well, I won't.

Exit **FLORENCE**. **AUSTIN** *sits down in desk-chair, staring at the wall, blankly.*

AUSTIN Metherell!

Enter from the ambulance-room **DR. WELLS**, *a young sporting doctor, nice-looking, with dark hair and moustache. He is passing through to the outer door.* **AUSTIN** *starts.*

Oh, it's you, Doctor. You startled me.

WELLS I beg your pardon, Mr. Whitworth.

AUSTIN My fault for day-dreaming. *(Rising)* Ready for contingencies in your torture chamber?

WELLS All clear. You look rather like a contingency yourself.

AUSTIN I'm—I'm nervous.

WELLS *(sympathetically)* It's a trying occasion. Don't you keep a bottle of whisky in that desk?

AUSTIN *(smiling)* Don't you know I do?

WELLS *(grinning)* I have some recollection of it. Take my strictly unprofessional advice and have a good strong nip.

AUSTIN *(at desk cupboard)* Have one yourself?

WELLS No, thanks. I'm going to look out for accidents.

AUSTIN Ghoul!

WELLS Every man to his trade.

Exit **WELLS**. **AUSTIN** *mixes drink. Enter* **EDMUND**.

EDMUND Hullo! That's bad, Austin.

AUSTIN Doctor's orders, Edmund. Will you?

EDMUND No, thanks.

AUSTIN How's the game?

EDMUND Rowdy. You're not watching it?

AUSTIN No. I'm praying for it.

EDMUND So far the gods have heard your prayer.

AUSTIN Metherell hasn't. I hear he's playing his best game against us.

EDMUND I'm no judge.

AUSTIN Are you tired of it already?

EDMUND I find it just a trifle wearing. Perhaps I'm too old to appreciate a new sensation. The excitement's too concentrated. And the noise! I'm deafened.

AUSTIN It's quiet enough in here. Those windows are double.

EDMUND They need to be. Austin, about Elsie.

AUSTIN Yes?

EDMUND And this footballer. You'll have to put your foot down.

AUSTIN I don't flatter myself I shall have much to say in the matter.

EDMUND Hang it, you're her father.

AUSTIN You heard what she said.

EDMUND To my blank astonishment, I did.

AUSTIN Oh, I'm used to it.

EDMUND Pull yourself together, Austin. You've drifted till your authority's flouted by your own children.

AUSTIN You know, Edmund, that sort of talk was all right in our day, but my children belong to the new generation, and the new generation regards parental authority as a played-out superstition.

EDMUND Nonsense. Be supine and they'll tread on you. You've only your own slackness to blame for it if you're flouted.

AUSTIN That, again, is the view of our time. We're old codgers to-day, Edmund, you and I.

EDMUND Confound it, Austin, you're not going to take this lying down!

AUSTIN No. I shall fight the fight of my generation against the next. I shall lose, of course.

EDMUND You mustn't lose.

AUSTIN Why should I be an exception to a natural law?

EDMUND Natural law! Natural laziness, you mean. You've simply let your children get out of hand through sheer weakness, and if you don't care to exert yourself to save Elsie from a gross *mésalliance*, I will.

AUSTIN Why's it a *mésalliance*?

EDMUND Good heavens, man—a footballer!

AUSTIN There spoke the acclimatized Londoner. Blackton won't be scandalized like Sevenoaks.

EDMUND Oh, hang your smug imitation democracy ! You don't believe that, Austin.

AUSTIN I always believe in the inevitable.

EDMUND It's not inevitable. It's incredible. Now, I'll tell you what I'll do, Austin. I'll take Elsie back with me to London and cure her of this infatuation with a jolly good round of the theatres and the shops.

AUSTIN My dear fellow! The theatres where she'll see nothing but romantic love stories and the shops where she'll go under your nose to buy her trousseau. Try it, Edmund. You'll be astonished at the result.

EDMUND It seems my *métier* to be astonished to-day. First I assist at an attempted bribery, and now it seems I'm to see my niece marry the incorruptible footballer.

AUSTIN You're a bachelor. The modern child surprises you. As a father, I have ceased to be surprised.

EDMUND As a father your idea of your duty is to stand idle while your daughter makes a sentimental mess of her life. I begin to thank my stars I'm a bachelor. At least I'm not henpecked by a rebellious family.

AUSTIN There's no rebellion about it, Edmund. I date from the sixties, they from the nineties, and we rub along quite peacefully in mutual toleration of the different attitudes.

EDMUND Tolerating the difference means that you give in to them every time.

AUSTIN Not quite.

EDMUND Then you won't give in to Elsie?

AUSTIN I shall be loyal to my generation, Edmund. She will be loyal to hers,—and youth will fight for her.

EDMUND That means you'll put up a protest for form's sake and give in gracefully when you think you've said enough to save your face.

AUSTIN No. Not if I can help it.

EDMUND Austin, you must help it. The thing's unthinkable. I'll help you to help it.

AUSTIN I shall be glad of any assistance you can give me.

> **AUSTIN** *turns a little wistfully to window.*

EDMUND You think I can't give much.

AUSTIN Hullo! The game's stopped. I hadn't heard the whistle go.

EDMUND I fancy I did a minute ago, without knowing its significance. What does it mean?

AUSTIN Probably an accident. Heaven help us if it's one of our men!

> *Enter* **WELLS** *and* **JACK***, who is in green-and-white football costume, soiled on the left side, with his left arm in an emergency sling.* **ELSIE** *follows.*

ELSIE *(anxiously)* Father, Jack's broken his arm.

WELLS Nothing very serious, Mr. Whitworth. I think it's only a simple fracture.

ELSIE Only!

WELLS *(taking* JACK *across)* Come along in here, Metherell. I'll have it set before you know where you are.

AUSTIN *(impulsively)* Metherell.

JACK *(as* WELLS *opens door)* Accidents will happen, Mr. Whitworth.

Exit WELLS *with him, closing door.*

ELSIE Doctors are callous beasts. *(She opens door and goes out with determination after them)*

AUSTIN *(scoffing)* Accident!

EDMUND Why not? Don't they happen?

AUSTIN After my proposition?

EDMUND He scorned it.

AUSTIN Second thoughts. I asked for bad play, but he's thinking of his reputation and he's broken his arm.

EDMUND Deliberately?

AUSTIN Yes.

EDMUND Heroic measures, Austin.

AUSTIN It's the last match of the season. He's all the summer months to get right in.

ELSIE *returns.*

ELSIE That doctor's turned me out.

AUSTIN Of course. You've no right in there.

ELSIE I've every right to be where Jack is suffering.

AUSTIN He can suffer very well without your assistance.

ELSIE You needn't be brutal about it, father.

AUSTIN I'm not being brutal. The man's a professional footballer. He accepts the risk of a broken limb as a part of his occupation. Metherell's not a wounded hero.

EDMUND No. He's simply a workman who'll doubtless receive proper compensation from his employers.

ELSIE And from me.

AUSTIN You!

ELSIE This will hurry on our marriage, father. Jack needs attention now.

AUSTIN Hasn't he got a mother?

ELSIE No mother could love him as I do. No one can nurse him as tenderly as I shall.

AUSTIN Nurse! A broken arm doesn't make an invalid of any one, especially a man in first-class physical condition.

ELSIE I think it's very cruel of you to belittle Jack's injuries.

EDMUND I wish you would stop calling him Jack.

ELSIE It's his name. He wasn't christened John.

EDMUND I refer to the impropriety of a young lady calling a workman by his Christian name.

ELSIE As the young lady is going to be married to the workman in the shortest possible time, I foil to see where the impropriety comes in.

EDMUND That is where we differ, my dear.

ELSIE About impropriety?

EDMUND No. About marriage.

ELSIE Would you rather I lived with him without being married?

AUSTIN Elsie!

ELSIE *(coolly)* Oh, it's all right, father. Uncle deserves a good shock. He's hopelessly suburban.

EDMUND *(pompously)* Elsie, I am older than you and—

ELSIE *(pertly)* Yes. That's your misfortune.

EDMUND *(angrily)* Will you allow me to speak without interrupting?

AUSTIN *sits in the armchair.*

ELSIE Yes, if you'll speak sensibly and won't put on side because your mind's grown old and pompous as well as your body.

AUSTIN Elsie, I won't have this rudeness to your uncle.

ELSIE My dear father, uncle is being stupid. The only way to combat stupidity is rudeness. Therefore, I am rude.

EDMUND *(humouring her)* I propose to speak sensibly according to my lights.

ELSIE *(under her breath)* Ancient lights.

EDMUND *(reasoning)* Now, suppose we do permit you to marry this—

ELSIE *(reproducing his reasonable tone)* Be careful, uncle. Talking of permission is on the border line.

EDMUND *(avoiding irritability)* Suppose you marry him, what interests can you have in common? I grant you he's a handsome specimen of manhood to-day, but retired athletes always run to seed.

AUSTIN *(self-consciously)* Hem!

EDMUND And apart from the attraction of the flesh, what's left?

ELSIE *(cordially)* Oh, you are talking sense this time. It's difficult, but I shall manage him.

EDMUND Shall you?

ELSIE *(confidently)* Oh yes. I couldn't do it if he were as old as you, because at your age a man's in a groove and sticks in it till he dies. Jack's not a modern, but he's young enough to learn. It's hardly credible, but at present he believes in Ruskin and Carlyle and reads Browning. Well, you know, I can't have a husband with a taste for Victorianism.

AUSTIN Then why have him at all?

ELSIE It's a curable disease.

EDMUND He reads Browning!

ELSIE Yes, but you needn't worry about that. I shall make a modern of him all right.

EDMUND Do you mean to tell me a footballer reads Browning?

ELSIE He can't always be at football. Oh yes. And Plato, only not in the original.

EDMUND Why, the man's a scholar.

ELSIE Did you think he was illiterate?

EDMUND I'm afraid I have underrated him. Still, that only proves him an estimable member of his class. It doesn't alter the fact that his class isn't yours.

ELSIE *(hotly)* Class! What do I care for class? Elemental passions sweep away class distinctions.

EDMUND That's a high falutin' name for a flirtation with a footballer.

ELSIE It's a name I thought you'd understand. Personally I'd say I've got the sex clutch on and other things don't matter. Any more shots, uncle?

EDMUND You needn't flatter yourself you've talked me into consenting to this marriage.

ELSIE Nobody asked you, sir, she said.

EDMUND *(angrily)* Nobody—

ELSIE *(easily conversational)* Wouldn't it interest you to see how the game's going, uncle?

EDMUND *(relieved)* I think it would. But don't you think you've heard the last of me.

ELSIE *(sympathetically)* No, but you want time to think out a few more objections.

EDMUND I am going purely out of desire to witness the match.

   Exit EDMUND.

ELSIE *(looking after him)* Poor dear. He tried his best.

AUSTIN *(half rising)* And I am going to try now.

ELSIE *(pushing him gently back into chair and sitting on its arm)* Oh, I don't mind you. He tried like an outraged relation. You'll try like a pal.

AUSTIN No. I'm going to be firm.

ELSIE What a bore.

AUSTIN *(seriously)* You didn't expect me to be pleased about this, did you?

ELSIE *(pouting)* Why not, if I'm pleased? Jack isn't marrying you.

AUSTIN Nor you, if I can help it.

ELSIE But you can't help it, you know.

AUSTIN Oh, I'm quite aware the stern parent isn't my game. But as pals, Elsie—

ELSIE *(nestling up to him)* Yes, father, as pals.

AUSTIN As goose to goose, it's not the thing. Now, frankly, is Jack Metherell up to our weight?

ELSIE He's above it.

AUSTIN Above it?

ELSIE Certainly. The condescension's his. He's a better footballer than ever you were, and you were no fool at football.

AUSTIN Football isn't everything, Elsie!

ELSIE Well, you play a decent hand at Bridge, but that's not much. Your golfs rotten. What else do you do well?

AUSTIN *(pushing her aside, and rising)* Really, Elsie!

ELSIE *(still an the arm)* Don't say "really." Tell me.

AUSTIN I hope I'm fairly good at being a gentleman.

ELSIE Doing, I said, not being.

AUSTIN *(humbly)* I—er—play the piano, you know.

ELSIE Yes, but you're not a musician within the meaning of the Act. You play the piano like a third-rate professional, too good for a public-house and not good enough for the concert platform, whereas Jack's football makes him a certainty for the England team in any international match. You may have more money than he has—

AUSTIN *(glancing at window)* I'm not even sure of that.

ELSIE *(triumphantly)* Then you've absolutely nothing on your side except a stupid and obsolete class prejudice.

AUSTIN Upon my word, Elsie—

ELSIE *(coming to him, gently)* Yes, I know I'm crushing, dear.

AUSTIN You're pitiless. Youth always is.

ELSIE Not always, father, but you shouldn't try to argue about love.

AUSTIN I was arguing about marriage.

ELSIE *(away from him)* I suppose at your age it's natural to be cynical about marriage and pretend it's nothing to do with love. And then of course when you were young it used to be the fashion to mock at marriage. We take our duties to society seriously to-day.

AUSTIN Are you proposing to marry Jack from a sense of duty?

ELSIE *(wistfully)* You'll be awfully proud of your grandchildren, father. They'll be most beautiful babies.

AUSTIN You look ahead, young woman.

ELSIE It's just as well I do. You're still worrying about a thing I settled weeks ago.

AUSTIN Then why didn't you tell me weeks ago?

ELSIE I hadn't told Jack then.

> **WELLS** *opens door, and enters with* **JACK,** *whose arm is in a splint and sling.*

WELLS *(entering)* You'd better go straight home now. Never mind about the match. I want you to avoid excitement for a while.

JACK The match doesn't excite me.

WELLS Then you can leave it without regret.

JACK *(indicating his costume)* In these?

WELLS I'll go round to the dressing-room and bring your clothes here if you'll trust me not to pick your pockets.

JACK There's nothing to pick. I've more sense than to take money into a dressing-tent.

AUSTIN Can't you trust the others, Metherell?

JACK *(drily)* Yes, so long as they're not tempted.

WELLS I won't be long. *(Exit)*

ELSIE *(watching* **WELLS** *resentfully till he goes)* Did he hurt you much, Jack?

JACK Not to speak of.

ELSIE *watches her scornfully.*

ELSIE Oh, you're brave. But you shall come to no more harm. I'll see you home safely.

AUSTIN *(sarcastically, indicating door of the ambulance-room)* You'll find cotton wool in there.

ELSIE What for?

AUSTIN To wrap him up in.

ELSIE Don't be spiteful, father.

AUSTIN Good heavens, girl, a broken arm is nothing.

JACK *sits wearily.*

ELSIE Except that the arm happens to be Jack's.

AUSTIN The civilized world will gasp at the great event.

ELSIE The athletic world certainly will. It's all very well for you to joke. Your arm's not hurt. It's all a gain to you. If Blackton don't win with only ten men against them, they deserve shooting. This accident means a lot.

AUSTIN I know what it means—better than you do. *(Looking at JACK)*

JACK *(jerking his head up)* What's that?

AUSTIN As you tactfully remarked, Metherell, accidents will happen.

JACK *(rising)* Don't you believe it was an accident?

ELSIE What else could it be? Do you think he broke his arm for fun?

JACK *(straight at AUSTIN)* It was an accident.

AUSTIN No, my lad. It was a bargain.

JACK I made no bargain.

AUSTIN *(sneering)* But you broke your arm.

JACK By acccident.

AUSTIN A singularly opportune coincidence.

ELSIE Father, what do you mean?

AUSTIN You'd better ask Metherell that.

ELSIE *(in puzzled appeal)* Jack!

JACK I'll say nothing.

ELSIE Then what am I to think?

JACK Think what you like.

ELSIE I think you're a sportsman, Jack, and—

AUSTIN I've known a sportsman do a bigger thing than break his arm for a woman.

ELSIE *(suspiciously)* A woman! What woman?

AUSTIN You, my dear. And, as you said, Blackton are sale to win now.

WELLS, *entering with* JACK'*s clothes and boots, overhears* AUSTIN.

WELLS I'm not so sure of that, Mr. Whitworth. It's anybody's game. The score's one all.

AUSTIN *(startled)* Birchester have scored!

WELLS Yes. Didn't you know? I'll look after Metherell. You're missing a good game.

ELSIE Then you'd better go and watch it, Dr. Wells.

WELLS *(slightly surprised)* I will when I've helped Metherell to change.

JACK I'm in no hurry. Don't put yourself about for me. Half time 'ull do.

WELLS Well, it can't be far off that now. *(Putting* JACK'*s clothes over chair)* I should like to see something of this match. Is the arm painful?

JACK It's sharpish.

WELLS *(by desk)* Pull yourself together with a dose of this. *(Lifting whisky bottle)*

JACK No, thanks. I'm a teetotaller.

AUSTIN *is lighting a cigar.*

WELLS *(authoritatively)* And I'm a doctor, man.

JACK That doesn't help my principles.

WELLS Oh, all right. If you like to be stubborn. Are you coming, Mr. Whitworth? *(Crossing to door)*

ELSIE Yes. Do go, father. They'll be expecting to see you outside.

AUSTIN *(grim)* Yes—I'm going—to show them I can smile. Come along, Doctor.

Exeunt WELLS *and* AUSTIN.

ELSIE Now, Jack. What's this all about?

JACK Your father's making a mistake.

ELSIE About what?

JACK *(exasperated)* It's a confidential matter, Elsie.

ELSIE That means there's something you're afraid to tell me.

JACK I'm not afraid. He spoke to me in private, and it's giving him away.

ELSIE You can't give him away to me. I've lived at home too long for that.

JACK I can't abuse his confidence.

ELSIE Are you going to talk about your conscience again? Father said you broke your arm for my sake and I want to know what it means.

JACK But I didn't, Elsie. It was an accident.

ELSIE He thought not.

JACK Yes. He's wrong.

ELSIE Why should he think you did it intentionally?

JACK *(sullenly)* Ask him.

ELSIE He's just told me to ask you. Now stop being absurd, Jack, and tell me all about it.

JACK (*reluctantly*) I told him we wanted to be married—

ELSIE *nods, smiling approval.*

—and he offered to strike a bargain. He wants Blackton to win, so I was to play a rotten game for Birchester.

ELSIE And you couldn't do it.

JACK No.

ELSIE (*enthusiastically*) No. You couldn't play badly if you tried, and so you broke your arm instead, for me. Jack, if I was proud of you before, I could worship you now. (*Patting the sling*) Your arm, your poor, hurt arm, mangled for me. My hero, my lover and my king.

JACK (*disgustedly*) You think that too!

ELSIE Think it! I know it. Don't pretend. It's too late now for modesty.

JACK Modesty! Don't you see if I'd done that, forgotten my sportsmanship and sold a match for my private gain, I'd deserve to be kicked round the county?

ELSIE No. I don't see it. You've hurt yourself for my sake, and that's enough to make of me the proudest woman in the land.

JACK It's enough to prove me dishonest if it were true.

ELSIE (*touching the arm*) Isn't that true?

JACK Don't I tell you that's an accident?

ELSIE You've never had an accident before.

JACK Not a serious one.

ELSIE No. You're too great a master of the game. Accidents happen to the careless and incompetent.

JACK Then I must be both. I fell and my arm twisted under me.

ELSIE And you really didn't do it on purpose?

JACK (*hurt*) Elsie, don't you believe me?

ELSIE It's so beastly to have to. I thought you were a perfect player, and you have an accident; and I thought you were a perfect lover, and you've been afraid to prove your love.

JACK (*stirred up*) Elsie, there are twenty thousand folk about this ground to-day and some of them have come to see the match, but more to see me play an honest game. They're just a football crowd, but there isn't a man upon this ground to-day but knows Jack Metherell is straight. It's left for you to say I ought to be a crook. You're great at golf and hockey. Is that the way you play the game?

ELSIE Forgive me, Jack. I did want things to be right for us.

JACK At any price?

ELSIE I'm sorry. I wasn't thinking of the game. I only thought of you.

JACK I know. But I want things to be right and rightly right.

ELSIE (*smiling*) And now they are.

JACK (*puzzled*) Your father—

ELSIE We've only to let him go on thinking you did it on purpose.

JACK But I didn't.

ELSIE (*soothingly*) I know. *I* know it was pure accident. But he doesn't.

JACK He must be told.

ELSIE I thought you wanted his consent to our marriage

JACK I do.

ELSIE Then let him think you've kept the bargain he proposed.

JACK Let him think I'm dishonest?

ELSIE What was he? What does it matter what he thinks if I know the truth?

JACK He's got to know the truth. If he'd have me as a scoundrel for your husband, he should be glad to have me as an honest man. (*Smiling sourly*) My arm's broke either way.

ELSIE I don't care tuppence for his consent.

JACK It's not the square thing to get married without.

ELSIE Oh, leave him to me.

JACK You bustle him so. It's not respectful, Elsie.

ELSIE Well, you needn't take him under your wing as well. It's not the custom in this family to split hairs about filial piety. I'll make it all right, Jack.

JACK It's my job, Elsie.

ELSIE It's our job, and you've had your innings. Now it's mine. But I'm going to take you home first to your mother.

JACK But my mother doesn't know about you, yet.

ELSIE *(drily)* It's time I made her acquaintance.

JACK *(doubtfully)* I don't know what she'll say.

ELSIE We'll find out when she says it. You think a peat deal of your mother, Jack.

JACK My father's dead. She's both to me. That's why I'm anxious.

ELSIE Anxious! But your mother wouldn't stop us, Jack.

JACK *(doubtfully)* You will be careful with her, Elsie.

ELSIE Careful?

JACK Yes. Not like you go on with your father. She's used to my way.

She has his unhurt arm, urging him to door, when it opens and **AUSTIN**, **FLORENCE** *and* **LEO** *enter.*

AUSTIN Still here, Metherell!

ELSIE I'm just going to take him home.

AUSTIN *(to* **JACK***)* Wasn't the doctor going to help you into your clothes? *(To* **LEO** *and* **FLORENCE***)* Where is Wells? Have either of you seen him?

LEO Last seen disappearing in the direction of the bar with an eminent London solicitor.

ELSIE Oh, never mind him. Jack's clothes can follow. We'll take a taxi.

AUSTIN But—

ELSIE Come along, Jack.

Exeunt **ELSIE** *and* **JACK**.

LEO I say, father, it's a jolly rough game. This must be one of the referee's slack days or he'd pull Angus up sharp.

AUSTIN *(genially)* The score's two—one for Blackton, my boy.

FLORENCE Blackton play against the wind next half.

AUSTIN *(confidently)* The match is all right. I've something else to talk about to you two. You saw Metherell and Elsie?

LEO *(grinning)* Yes. It's a case.

AUSTIN What?

LEO *(the grin fading)* Well, isn't it?

AUSTIN So you know.

LEO I've got eyes.

AUSTIN You take it philosophically.

LEO I don't see that it matters how I take it.

AUSTIN To my mind it matters considerably. He'll be your brother-in-law if he marries her.

LEO That had occurred to me.

AUSTIN Don't you mind?

LEO I don't mind. Metherell's a stupendous nut at football.

AUSTIN I understood football didn't interest you

LEO Merely academically.

AUSTIN It's really far more your concern than mine, you know, Leo. In the natural course of things Elsie's husband will be your brother-in-law for a longer period than he'll be my son-in-law. Yours too, Flo.

FLORENCE Yes. *(Pause)*

AUSTIN *(exasperated)* Well? Have neither of you anything to say?

FLORENCE *(rather bored)* Not much in my line, dad.

LEO Nor in mine. As I'm her brother I can't cut the other fellow out and marry her myself. I'm rather thankful, too. Elsie takes a lot of stopping when she's got the bit between her teeth.

AUSTIN I don't get much help from you.

FLORENCE Why should you?

LEO It's no use jibbing, father. Much easier to give them your blessing and a cheque.

AUSTIN It is always easiest to give way, Leo.

LEO Yes. Isn't it?

AUSTIN *(wildly)* Good heavens, do you young people care about nothing?

LEO We're tremendously in earnest about a lot of things, only they're not the things you're in earnest about. There are fashions in shibboleths just as much as in socks, and you're a little out of date in both.

AUSTIN Possibly. But blood is still thicker than water, Leo Metherell is a man of the people and—

LEO Oh, my dear father, don't talk about the people as if they inhabited an inferior universe. The class bogey is one of the ghosts we've laid to-day.

AUSTIN Indeed. I'd an idea it was rather rampant.

LEO I believe it used to be. As a matter of fact, I do object to Metherell.

AUSTIN Oh! You have some sense left.

FLORENCE I don't. I only wish I was in Elsie's shoes.

LEO Was I speaking, Flo, or were you?

FLORENCE You were, too much.

LEO I object theoretically on esthetic grounds because of the destined fatness of the retired footballer. But I have Elsie's assurance that Metherell's a teetotaller and I trust her to give him a lively enough time to keep him decently thin, so that practically my objection falls to pieces.

AUSTIN Leo, I didn't expect much help from you, but upon my word your cynicism is disgusting.

LEO I expect, you know, that's pretty much what grandfather thought of you.

Enter **ELSIE** *and* **JACK**.

Hullo! are there no taxis?

ELSIE *(angry)* I think every taxi in the town is outside the ground, but the men are too keen on getting a free sight of the game from the roofs of their cabs to take a fare.

FLORENCE It's a sporting town, Blackton.

LEO I should have thought they'd take it as an honour to drive Metherell home.

JACK *(bitterly)* Not in the Birchester colours.

LEO *(sarcastically)* Sporting town, Blackton.

ELSIE *(at white heat)* They're beasts. Beasts. They jeered. They're glad he's hurt.

JACK That's what you've done for me, Mr. Whitworth. I'm laughed at in Blackton. Last Saturday I was their idol, and now—

AUSTIN You've done it for yourself, my boy.

JACK *(hotly)* You transferred me.

AUSTIN I meant the broken arm, not the broken idol.

JACK *(scornfully)* Do you still think I did it purposely?

AUSTIN I don't think, Metherell. I know. And I'm very much obliged to you. The chances are it's won the match.

JACK *(sulkily)* It *was* an accident.

AUSTIN *(playing his last card)* Oh, you needn't keep that up before the family. That reminds me. *(Turning to them)* Leo, Florence, this is your future brother-in-law, Jack Metherell, the sporting footballer, who's sold a match to buy my consent to his marrying Elsie.

He watches LEO *and* FLORENCE *for the effect.* JACK *steps forward, but* ELSIE *stops him.*

ELSIE Hush, Jack.

FLORENCE *(coldly)* I don't believe it, father. That consenting business went out with the flood.

LEO *(to* JACK*)* Did you ask my father's consent?

JACK Yes.

LEO It's just credible, Flo.

FLORENCE In England? In the twentieth century?

LEO These quaint old customs linger. Half the world doesn't know how the other half thinks.

AUSTIN *(who has been looking on amazed)* But aren't you horrified?

LEO At his asking? No. Merely interested in the survival of an archaism.

AUSTIN At his selling a match, man!

LEO A man who would ask papa is capable of anything.

ELSIE He's not capable of dishonesty.

AUSTIN Oh, you're blind with love.

ELSIE I have his word.

AUSTIN *(scoffing)* His word!

ELSIE Yes. Jack Metherell's word. The word of the man I'm going to marry.

AUSTIN *(indicating* JACK*'s arm)* Deeds speak louder than words.

JACK *(with resolution)* Yes, Mr. Whitworth, they do. You think you've won this match. We'll see.

ELSIE *(frightened)* Jack, what are you going to do?

JACK Play. Play for Birchester as I've never played for Blackton. I'll show him if I sold the match.

LEO No. I say. You mustn't do that with a broken arm.

JACK Yes. Broken arm and all.

LEO It's madness. Look here, I believe you. So does Elsie.

FLORENCE And I.

LEO We all do, except father, and I assure you he's subject to hallucinations. Thinks he can play the piano. Thinks my poetry's bad. Thinks you're a rotter. All sorts of delusions.

JACK *(stubbornly)* Birchester must win. I'm going on that field to show them all what football is.

As he speaks **WELLS** *and* **EDMUND** *enter.*

WELLS *(with calm authority)* I think not, Metherell.

JACK Out of my way, Doctor.

WELLS I forbid it.

JACK Much I care for your forbidding.

WELLS One moment, Metherell. The play is extraordinarily rough. It's Blackton's game to lame their opponents.

EDMUND More like a shambles than a game.

WELLS *(to* **AUSTIN**) The referee is strangely kind to Blackton, Mr. Whitworth.

AUSTIN Oh?

JACK *(suspiciously)* What? What's that you said?

WELLS I say if I were referee I'd have ordered off half the Blackton team for rough play. This is no match for a damaged man, Metherell.

JACK So you did try the referee, Mr. Whitworth.

AUSTIN I don't understand you.

JACK Don't you? Well, rough or smooth, I'm going through it now. *(To* **WELLS**) Thanks for your warning. *(To* **AUSTIN**) And I warn *you* that referee had best be careful now, or I'll report him.

ELSIE *(holding him)* For my sake, Jack.

JACK *(gently shaking her off)* It is for your sake, Elsie, not for his. His consent's nothing to me after this. My record's going to be clean.

Exit JACK.

AUSTIN *(rubbing his hands)* Ah! Splendid. Edmund, I've brought you down from town for nothing. The match is ours.

EDMUND *(drily)* Then I can devote my undivided attention to the problem of my niece. But why's the match yours?

AUSTIN Metherell is kind enough to give it us. An injured player is a nuisance to his side—no use and only in the way.

ELSIE You don't know Jack.

AUSTIN Oh yes, I do. You think he's a hero. I know he's a fool.

ELSIE Then he's an honest fool, and—

AUSTIN I haven't time to argue the point now. I want a word with the referee before the game recommences. *(Going)*

ELSIE So Jack was right. You did bribe the referee!

AUSTIN Elsie, if you don't want us all to starve, you'll keep a tight hold of your tongue.

LEO Starve!

ELSIE Starve! What—

AUSTIN Oh, ask your uncle.

ELSIE I haven't time. I'm going to Jack's home to see that all's prepared for him.

AUSTIN Oh, go to—Go where you like.

ELSIE I usually do.

Exit AUSTIN.

EDMUND Now, Elsie, about this footballer.

ELSIE *(moving)* I shall be rather busy turning his bedroom into a hospital for the next hour, uncle.

EDMUND You're to do nothing so compromising.

ELSIE *(scornfully)* Compromising!

EDMUND If you insist on going, I shall come with you.

ELSIE You will look funny in Elizabeth Street.

EDMUND I prefer to look ridiculous than that you should look indiscreet.

LEO *(at window, crossing)* There's the whistle. Come along, Flo.

FLORENCE Yes. They're playing.

Exeunt **FLORENCE** *and* **LEO**.

ELSIE You mean to come?

EDMUND I don't mean you to go alone.

ELSIE I wish you were in London, uncle. Your intentions are so good.

Curtain

ACT THREE

At 41, Elizabeth Street (he combined kitchen and living-room opens directly to the street, the street door being centre, with the window next to it Through the window the other side of the drab street is seen. A door leads to the stairs, while another gives access to the scullery. The room is fairly comfortable. A handsome presentation clock is on the mantel over the fireplace. The plate-rack is well furnished. Rocking-chair by fireplace. Sofa under window, behind which is a plant on a stand. Table round which three **OLD WOMEN** *sit at tea.* **MRS. WILMOT** *and* **MRS. NORBURY**, *as visitors, wear outdoor clothes and bonnets, of which they have loosened the strings.* **MRS. METHERELL** *has grey hair, a small person, and an indomitable will. She is too hearty to be ill-natured, but she is mistress of her house and knows it. She wears her after-work dress of decent black. The remains of a substantial meal are on the table. Smoke-blackened kettle on fire.*

MRS. WILMOT *(sighing)* Eh, yes. Elizabeth Street isn't what it was.

MRS. METHERELL It's not the street, Amy, it's the people in it.

MRS. NORBURY It used to be known for a saving street when I first came to live here. Every house had a bank-book

MRS. WILMOT And there's more money coming into the street to-day than there was then.

MRS. NORBURY And going out. They spend more in an ordinary week than ever me and my old man spent in a holiday week one time, and if they don't spend, they gamble, and nothing to show for it all at the finish.

MRS. WILMOT Yes, and come begging off their mother as soon as they fall sick or out of work. And that uppish with it all!

MRS. NORBURY Do you think I can get my girls to stay at home and give me a lift with the house of an evening? Not they. They've always something on that's more important than me. I'm nobody. And the money those girls spend on their clothes!

MRS. WILMOT Time was when a man 'ud come straight home when he'd finished work and be satisfied with doing a bit in his garden. Most he'd ever think of, barring Saturday night of course, was one night a week at his club, Nowadays it's every night the same.

MRS. METHERELL *moves impatiently.*

MRS. NORBURY I know. You did know where to lay your hand on them once, but there's no telling where they get to now.

MRS. WILMOT It's all these picture shows and music halls.

MRS. METHERELL *(roughly)* It's all your own fault, Amy.

MRS. WILMOT Why?

MRS. METHERELL You let them put upon you.

MRS. NORBURY I suppose you don't?

MRS. METHERELL Our Jack doesn't carry on that road.

MRS. WILMOT He'll have it out of you yet. He's quiet and deep.

MRS. METHERELL *(confidently)* He's safe enough.

MRS. WILMOT Till he breaks out.

MRS. METHERELL He's never broken yet.

MRS. NORBURY You're lucky, then.

MRS. METHERELL It isn't luck. It's the way you go about it with them.

MRS. NORBURY *(enviously)* Yours gets good money, too.

MRS. METHERELL And I see it all. We've a use for a bank-book in this house.

MRS. WILMOT I wish I saw the half of what mine get. Always crying out for more, but not to give it me. Some of them wouldn't be happy if they'd their own motor-car.

MRS. METHERELL Yes. That's the way. When I was young a man could start poor and end rich. He'd save and stick to what he got. These lads to-day 'ull never rise. They're too busy spending what they have. My Jack knows a game worth two of that. He's improving his mind. His bedroom's full of books. Fitting himself to rise, Jack is.

MRS. NORBURY There are a few like that. They're rare and scarce.

Knock at street door.

(she rises) I'm nearest.

MRS. METHERELL *(rising)* Sit you still. *(Crosses and opens door)*

ELSIE *and* EDMUND *are there.*

EDMUND Mrs. Metherell?

MRS. METHERELL *(gruffly)* Yes?

Immediately on the "Yes," ELSIE *enters past her.*

EDMUND May we come in?

MRS. METHERELL Looks as if you were in.

EDMUND *enters hesitatingly.*

ELSIE Have you heard about Jack's accident?

MRS. WILMOT *and* MRS. NORBURY *remain seated, eyeing* ELSIE*'s clothes.*

MRS. METHERELL *(closing door calmly)* Yes. There was a special out. They get papers out for anything nowadays.

ELSIE *(indignantly)* You take it very easily.

MRS. METHERELL He'll be looked after. There's a doctor on the ground.

EDMUND *(politely awkward)* Perhaps I ought to introduce myself, Mrs. Metherell. My name is Whitworth—Mr. Austin Whitworth's brother. This is Miss Whitworth.

MRS. METHERELL *(with some anxiety)* Is Jack hurt worse?

ELSIE *(gravely)* Not that we *know* of.

MRS. WILMOT *(rising)* I think we'd best be going.

MRS. METHERELL No. It's all right.

MRS. NORBURY *(rising and tying bonnet-strings)* I can see we're not wanted. We'll be seeing you again before you flit to Birchester.

MRS. METHERELL *(by door with them)* Many a time. We don't go yet. *(Opening door)*

MRS. WILMOT Good-bye.

MRS. METHERELL Good-bye.

Exeunt **MRS. WILMOT** *and* **MRS. NORBURY**. **MRS. METHERELL** *closes door and turns to* **ELSIE**.

Now, what is it ? If it's bad news I can stand it.

ELSIE Is Jack's bed prepared?

MRS. METHERELL *(righteously indignant)* Jack's bed was made at eight o'clock this morning. Do you take me for a slut?

ELSIE Oh yes, but he'll need special nursing, and the room—which is his room? *(Looking at doors left and right)*

MRS. METHERELL *(drily)* His room's upstairs.

ELSIE I'm going to see that it's right.

MRS. METHERELL His room's my job.

ELSIE Yes, yes. I know. But I must make sure. Don't you realize he's gone on playing with a broken arm?

MRS. METHERELL He was always a fool. But he's not so soft as to take to his bed for a damaged arm.

ELSIE *(wildly)* Anything may have happened. Complications. Fever. I'm going to his room. Which is it, please?

MRS. METHERELL *(guarding the door)* You're not going.

ELSIE I am. Please don't be stupid, Mrs. Metherell.

EDMUND Elsie!

MRS. METHERELL Do you think I'll have a girl I've never set eyes on before ferreting round my house?

ELSIE But—oh, you tell her, uncle. *(Darts past* **MRS. METHERELL** *and exit)*

MRS. METHERELL *(calling after her)* Here, you come back. Cheek!

EDMUND I think perhaps in the circumstances, Mrs. Metherell—

MRS. METHERELL *(with the door handle in her hand)* What circumstances?

EDMUND Don't you know about my niece?

MRS. METHERELL I know she's a forward hussy, like most young girls to-day. That's all I know.

EDMUND Then I must explain.

MRS. METHERELL *(glancing off)* You'd better.

EDMUND You see, she and your son are engaged to be married.

MRS. METHERELL *(pausing, astonished, then closing door)* It's the first I've heard of it.

EDMUND *(pleased to find her hostile)* Perhaps I ought rather to say they think they're engaged.

MRS. METHERELL No. You oughtn't. Jack doesn't think he's tied to any woman till he's told me first and got my leave.

EDMUND *(delighted)* Ah, now that's quite splendid, Mrs. Metherell. I'm glad to find that you agree with me.

MRS. METHERELL In what?

EDMUND In opposing the engagement.

MRS. METHERELL Why do you?

EDMUND *(easily)* Well, on grounds, shall we say, of general unsuitability.

MRS. METHERELL I don't oppose. *(Sitting in rocking-chair)*

EDMUND *remains standing.*

EDMUND I understood—

MRS. METHERELL I don't know owt about the girl. She's made a bad start with me, but she's excited and I'll give fair play. She may be good enough for Jack. I cannot tell you yet. What makes you think she isn't?

EDMUND I didn't exactly think that.

MRS. METHERELL What did you think? Out with it, You're her uncle, you know more about the girl than I can.

EDMUND Well, the fact is I don't consider she would be a suitable wife for your son.

MRS. METHERELL That's what you said before. I want to know why not. Has she a temper?

EDMUND *(on his dignity)* Certainly not.

MRS. METHERELL Flirts then? Not steady? Extravagant?

EDMUND No, no.

MRS. METHERELL Well, is she deformed or does she drink?

EDMUND Good heavens, woman, no.

MRS. METHERELL If you won't tell me what's wrong with her, I must find out for myself.

EDMUND There is nothing wrong with her.

MRS. METHERELL Then, where's your objection?

EDMUND My objection, stated explicitly, is— *(Hesitating)*

MRS. METHERELL Yes? Go on.

EDMUND I find it rather difficult to explain to you.

MRS. METHERELL I've a thick skin.

EDMUND *(desperately)* My niece's training and upbringing do not make her a fit wife for your son, Mrs. Metherell.

MRS. METHERELL Did you make a mess of her upbringing?

EDMUND No, but—

MRS. METHERELL How did you bring her up?

EDMUND As a lady.

MRS. METHERELL Then she's handicapped for life. But I have seen some grow out of it.

Enter **ELSIE**. *She has a towel over her arm.*

ELSIE Mrs. Metherell, will you come upstairs a minute?

MRS. METHERELL What for?

ELSIE We ought to have hot water ready and I can't find the bath-room.

MRS. METHERELL You'd have a job to find one in Elizabeth Street.

ELSIE *(blankly)* How do you get hot water?

MRS. METHERELL *(drily)* You heat it.

EDMUND *stands, looking on.*

ELSIE *(crossing to fireplace and making for kettle)* Then I'll take this.

MRS. METHERELL *(rising and getting kettle first)* That's for his tea. *(Glancing at clock, kettle in hand)* I'll make it too. He always comes in hungry from a match. *(She replaces kettle, takes tea-pot from table, empties the used tea-leaves behind the fire, fills generously from canister on mantel and makes tea, replacing kettle and leaving tea-pot on the hob)*

ELSIE Oh, what have you got for him? He'll need nourishing.

MRS. METHERELL There's a bit of steak-pie in the cupboard left over from dinner. He'll have it cold.

ELSIE But meat is so indigestible with tea, and he's an invalid.

EDMUND *sits on sofa.*

MRS. METHERELL Eh, stop moithering, lass. You don't know owt about it. *(Suddenly noticing)* What's that over your arm?

ELSIE Oh, I'm sorry. It was upstairs.

MRS. METHERELL That's my towel when you've done with it. *(Takes it, then surprised)* Where did you get this from?

ELSIE The bedroom.

MRS. METHERELL That's one of my best towels. It isn't out of Jack's room.

ELSIE I've arranged the front bedroom for him.

MRS. METHERELL *(angrily)* I'd have you to know that's my room.

ELSIE The other is such a cheerless, poky little place. It's dark, there's no fireplace, no proper carpet, nothing but a camp-bed and a second-hand bookstall.

MRS. METHERELL It's good enough for him.

ELSIE Nothing but the best is good enough for a man who plays football like Jack.

MRS. METHERELL Football's one thing. Home's another. He's at home here. Do you think he sleeps in the best bedroom?

ELSIE He must have the best-lighted room just now.

MRS. METHERELL So I'm to turn out for him. am I?

ELSIE That isn't asking very much. I don't believe you care for him at all. How can you sit at home when he's playing football?

MRS. METHERELL Custom's everything. *(Sitting in rocking-chair)* I'm used to my men being before the public. Jack's father was a public man—an undertaker, *(EDMUND winces)* and I've known him have as many as six funerals on a Saturday afternoon, but I didn't go to the cemetery to see he buried them properly, and I reckon it's the same with Jack. He can kick a ball without my watching him. *(Changing tone)* And now perhaps you'll tell me what you mean by interfering in my house?

ELSIE *(to EDMUND)* Haven't you told her, uncle?

EDMUND Oh yes. I told her.

ELSIE *(smilingly sure of herself)* Well, Mrs. Metherell, will I do? *(Standing before her)*

MRS. METHERELL *(still sitting)* You said yourself just now that nothing but the best is good enough for Jack, so you'll excuse my being particular. I've been asking your uncle about you and he tells me you're a lady, born and bred.

ELSIE You mustn't blame me for my relations, Mrs. Metherell.

MRS. METHERELL Nay, I don't. Mine's a respectable family, but there's a Metherell doing time at this moment, and another to my certain knowledge who ought to be. But this is where it comes in. If you're going to be Jack's wife, you've to know your way about a house.

ELSIE *(agreeing)* Yes.

MRS. METHERELL Your father 'ull keep a servant, I suppose.

ELSIE Oh, but I do my share. Servants require a lot of management.

MRS. METHERELL *(dryly)* I'll take your word for it. I never had any. And Jack 'ull have none, either.

ELSIE I didn't expect it.

MRS. METHERELL *(graciously)* You may be handier than you look. I'll try. Those pots want washing. Let me see you shape.

ELSIE *eagerly begins to put the used cups together.*

There's a tray. *(Pointing to plate-rack)* The sink's in yonder. *(Pointing)*

EDMUND *(protesting)* Really, Mrs. Metherell— *(He rises)*

ELSIE It's all right, uncle. *(The tray is loaded and she lifts it)* In there, Mrs. Metherell? *(Starting to go)*

MRS. METHERELL Yes.

EDMUND *opens door.* ELSIE *is going through.*

That'll not do. You won't have a man about the place to wait on you. Close that door, Mr. Whitworth, and let me see her get out by herself.

EDMUND *closes it, and comes away.* ELSIE *tries to open it, the tray is troublesome and the pots slip together on it.* MRS. METHERELL *rises and crosses rapidly.*

Those are my cups, you know. Here, give it to me. *(Takes tray and exit, opening door with the ease of familiarity)*

ELSIE I'm sorry, Mrs. Metherell. But I can learn.

MRS. METHERELL *(offstage)* Maybe. You've shown willing. *(She closes door from outside)*

EDMUND Come away, Elsie. You've seen enough of the Metherell standard to show you it will never do.

ELSIE *(her confidence a little shaken, but still fighting)* I shall alter the standard.

EDMUND It's fixed. You can't alter it. It's impossible.

ELSIE The modern eye is blind to impossibilities. Have you ever been to an Ideal Home Exhibition?

EDMUND A what?

ELSIE They show you little houses fitted up with the cutest dodges for saving labour. I know Mrs. Metherell will have to make her home with us, but it'll be a very different home from this. You can credit me with some imagination.

EDMUND I do, if you think Mrs. Metherell will ever believe her house is clean unless she or some one else has drudged in it all day. Seeing's believing, and you can't see the dust fly in a vacuum cleaner.

ELSIE She'll have to use her common sense.

EDMUND The scrubbing brush survives in spite of common sense.

Enter JACK, *dressed as Act I., left arm in splint. He opens and enters without knocking, but he hasn't time to get his cap off before* ELSIE *is with him.*

ELSIE You're safe.

JACK And sound, too, but for this. *(Glancing at his arm)*

ELSIE *(hysterically)* Thank God.

EDMUND Is the match over?

JACK Three—two for Birchester.

EDMUND *(distressed)* Birchester have won!

JACK I won the match for Birchester, if it gives you any satisfaction to know it. I haven't been a man. I've been a miracle.

ELSIE You always were.

JACK I've only done my human best before to-day, To-day I've been a superman, a thing inspired, protected guarded by a greater mastery than I have ever known. It wasn't football as it is in life. It's been the football of my dreams.

EDMUND It makes you talk.

JACK I'm still intoxicated with the glamour of that game.

EDMUND Yes, Metherell, success is sweet. But somebody is suffering for this.

ELSIE Who?

EDMUND If Birchester have won, Blackton have lost.

ELSIE For an outsider, you take it seriously.

EDMUND I take it seriously for your father. I ought to be with him now.

ELSIE Haven't you done enough here for the proprieties?

EDMUND I must go to your father, Elsie. Come.

ELSIE I stay here with Jack.

EDMUND *(after a struggle)* Very well.

Exit **EDMUND**.

JACK *(taking cap off)* Elsie, what are you doing here?

ELSIE I came to—to see your mother.

JACK You've told her about us?

ELSIE Yes.

JACK It should have come from me. She'd expect that. But no matter, now she knows. What did she say?

ELSIE *(hesitating, then plunging)* It's—it's all right, Jack.

JACK Hurrah! Then we've a clear road now. I was a bit afraid. Mother has a will of her own, and she's not easy to please. But I might have known she couldn't resist you. Tell me what she said when you pleaded to her with the loveliest eyes in the world and told her you loved me.

ELSIE *(awkwardly)* Well—

JACK *(interrupting enthusiastically)* Yes, I know—you needn't tell me. can see it all. You there, she here, and then you fell into each other's arms, and she kissed you, and what you said to each other I'm not to know, for it was women's talk not meant for men to hear.

ELSIE Jack, you've never been like this before.

JACK No, I've never played a great game with a broken arm and come through it unscathed. I've never—oh, but it's you that's done the greatest thing for me. You've won my mother for us. That was the cloud that used to get between.

ELSIE And made you talk of self-improvement instead of my eyes? It's only now I learn you know my eyes are good.

JACK I have always known the beauty of your eyes.

ELSIE You couldn't tell me about them.

JACK Not till it was all made right with mother, I thought last night to-day would be the saddest day I've known. I had to play for Birchester and go away from Blackton and from you. And there was mother, but you were brave and took that burden from me, and I'm glad, Elsie, I'm glad of everything.

ELSIE Even of that? *(Touching his arm)*

JACK It's brought me luck. It's brought me you, safely secure at last. I wish I had a dozen arms to break.

ELSIE *(smiling)* To get a dozen me's?

JACK To suffer with for you.

ELSIE *(quickly)* You are suffering?

JACK This bit of pain is nothing to a bad conscience, and it's that I had meeting you and knowing I'd not the pluck to have it out with mother. *(With a touch of brutality)* But now I've got you for my own. No, not a dozen of you, Elsie. One's good enough for me. *(He puts his arm round her, kissing roughly)*

ELSIE *(frightened)* Jack, you're very strong.

JACK *(squeezing masterfully)* I've only one arm, but it's strong.

ELSIE I love your strength, Jack, but you do take my breath away. You've never kissed me like that before.

JACK *(still holding her against her will)* I've not been free before. I've kissed you guiltily, not as a free man kisses when he can give his whole mind to it.

ELSIE Jack, let me go.

JACK Don't you like it? I said you'd be the first to tire of kissing.

ELSIE *(free of him)* It's—it's almost terrifying, Jack.

JACK *(roughly)* Rubbish, lass, you're not made of glass. You can stand it. I needn't kiss you like I kiss my mother.

ELSIE How do you kiss your mother?

JACK Why, respectfully.

ELSIE You don't respect me, then?

JACK It's not the same. I love you.

ELSIE *(rather more hopefully)* And you don't love her?

JACK It's different. Where is she now?

ELSIE *(indicating)* She went in there to wash some pots.

JACK *(nodding, anxiously)* She does too much of that. The work comes heavy at her age.

ELSIE We'll change all that.

JACK *(eagerly)* Yes. Four hands 'ull make it easy.

ELSIE My methods will be very different.

JACK Different? She'll not like changing her ways. Old people don't like change.

ELSIE *(callously)* No, but it's good for them.

JACK My getting married 'ull be change enough. We must be careful not to upset her.

ELSIE You're very fond of your mother, Jack.

JACK I try to do my duty.

ELSIE *(gladly)* It's only duty, then?

JACK Only! Honour thy father and thy mother that—

ELSIE Yes, but I don't want to make old bones. And that honouring business is a bit fly-blown. We spell it humour your parents nowadays and not too much of that. A badly brought up parent's worse than a spoilt child.

JACK Of course, you're joking, Elsie, and I know I'm not a judge of taste, but I don't somehow think we ought to make fun of our parents.

ELSIE I wasn't joking, Jack. If your mother's going to stay with us, she'll have to realize the century she's living in.

JACK *(reprovingly)* My mother's mistress of this house, Elsie.

ELSIE This house. Yes. But we're going to be happy in a cottage on the moors by Birchester, and if people who've forgotten what it is to be young try any interference, so much the worse for them.

JACK *(angrily)* Did you tell her that before you asked about the marrying?

ELSIE Tell her what?

JACK That you expected her to take a back seat and watch you interfering with her arrangements?

ELSIE Interfering's not the word. They'll be revolutionized. Our cottage will be run on rational and hygienic principles.

JACK I'd rather have it comfortable.

ELSIE It will be comfortable.

JACK With you and her squabbling all the time?

ELSIE *(very discouraged, but still brave)* We shan't squabble if she'll be sensible.

JACK Her idea of sense mayn't be the same as yours.

ELSIE It probably won't. It's all right, Jack. I've had practice in handling parents.

JACK I've seen a bit of it, too. You shan't treat mother that way. If we're to marry, Elsie—

ELSIE *If* we're to marry!

JACK My mother's first with me. I take my orders from her and you'll just have to do the same.

Enter **MRS. METHERELL**. *She has an apron on which she wipes her hands and then takes it off, hanging up behind door.*

MRS. METHERELL So you've broken your arm, I hear.

JACK *(his attitude is that of a weak-willed child. He almost cowers before her)* Yes, mother.

MRS. METHERELL   Wasn't there work enough with a flitting without fetching and carrying for you? Who's going to break the coals now?

ELSIE   Mrs. Metherell!

JACK   It's all right, Elsie. It's just her way.

MRS. METHERELL   *(turning on* ELSIE*)* And you've been turning my house upside down upstairs. A lot of need you have to talk, my girl. You've been in here ten minutes with a famished man and not so much as lifted a hand to put out his food. I told you where it was.

ELSIE   I'm sorry. *(Going in terrified alacrity to cupboard, and finding plate of cold steak pie, which she puts on table)*

MRS. METHERELL   *(with rough kindness)* Sit you down, Jack. *(Lifts teapot to table and pours)*

ELSIE   Oh, that tea's been made so long.

JACK   I like it black.

ELSIE   I'm sure Jack, ought to have—

MRS. METHERELL   Jack 'ull have what I provide for him, and be thankful he's got it.

ELSIE *fusses over* JACK*'s plate, cutting up small.*

ELSIE   *(to* JACK*)* You'll be having late dinners in a month.

MRS. METHERELL *is returning teapot to hob.*

JACK   She'll never let us.

MRS. METHERELL   *(returning)* I'll do that.

ELSIE *moves away.*

If he's to be spoon-fed, I'll feed him.

ELSIE   *(timidly)* I was doing it to help you, Mrs. Metherell.

MRS. METHERELL   You were doing it to show how fond you are. What's this I hear about you, Jack?

JACK   *(his mouth full)* Well, she's told you.

MRS. METHERELL   Hadn't you a tongue in your own mouth?

JACK I'd have told you to-night.

MRS. METHERELL Going courting behind my back.

JACK You will have your grumble, mother.

MRS. METHERELL I'd do more than grumble if you hadn't gone
and hurt yourself. You might have done it on purpose just
to get on the soft side of me.

ELSIE Is this your soft side, Mrs. Metherell?

MRS. METHERELL Yes. Company manners. I'm keeping what
I have to say to Jack till you've gone.

ELSIE Jack's ill. You're not to bully him.

MRS. METHERELL Is he your son or mine? Because if he's mine
I'll not ask your leave to say what I like to him. I'm mistress
here.

ELSIE Yes, but, Mrs. Metherell—

MRS. METHERELL That'll do from you. I've had enough of your
back answers. You talk too much.

Knock at door. MRS. METHERELL, *eyeing* ELSIE *as she goes,
opens door.* AUSTIN *is outside.*

AUSTIN Mrs. Metherell?

MRS. METHERELL Yes.

ELSIE *(coming forward on hearing the voice)* Father!

AUSTIN You here, Elsie! *(Entering—to* MRS. METHERELL*)* Thank
you.

MRS. METHERELL *closes door grimly.*

Well, Metherell, I've come to see how you are.

JACK *(rising)* I wasn't carried off the field, but it isn't you I have
to thank for it.

AUSTIN *(sincerely)* No. It's your own magnificent skill. I never saw
such play.

MRS. METHERELL *(coming between them)* You'll excuse me, but
I don't allow that kind of talk in here.

AUSTIN *(surprised)* But I was praising your son, Mrs. Metherell.

MRS. METHERELL He's buttered up too much outside. In here he get's his makeweight of the other thing.

JACK There's no more praise for me in this town, mother. I'm not popular. They've lost a lot of money on this match.

MRS. METHERELL Was that your fault?

JACK I played for Birchester. The bets were made on Blackton before they knew I was transferred.

MRS. METHERELL *(indignantly)* They're blaming *you* for that?

AUSTIN Fair weather sportsmen!

JACK There's no denying I won the match for Birchester.

MRS. METHERELL *(indignantly)* Whose fault was it you played for Birchester? Yours? No. There stands the man you have to thank for that.

AUSTIN *(taken aback)* Really, Mrs. Metherell, I was hardly prepared—

MRS. METHERELL *(accusingly)* You've made my Jack unpopular. That's what you've done. *(Looking at* **JACK** *proudly, while he expresses blank astonishment)* There never was a favourite like Jack. Not a man in the whole of Blackton but looked up to Jack, nor a woman but envied me my son.

JACK But, mother, I didn't know you cared. You've always—

MRS. METHERELL You didn't know I cared! Because I haven't gone and shouted with the others round the field, because I haven't dinned it in your ears and did my level best to stop them spoiling you, do you think I took no pride in knowing you're the idol of the town? I'll show you if I care. Out of that door, Mr. Whitworth. Out of that door, I say. You've brought trouble on this house.

AUSTIN Really, this is very embarrassing.

MRS. METHERELL I'll embarrass you. You've made my Jack unpopular. What do you want here? Your daughter? Take her and go.

AUSTIN What I wanted was a little private conversation with your son, Mrs Metherell.

MRS. METHERELL You've finished with my son. You're not his master now.

AUSTIN No. But as a friend, I hoped—

MRS. METHERELL And you're not his friend.

AUSTIN I can't make things clear if you won't let met Mrs. Metherell.

MRS. METHERELL They're clear enough.

AUSTIN *(desperately)* Metherell, will you do me the favour of stepping outside with me for three minutes' business conversation?

MRS. METHERELL *(scoffing)* Business!

ELSIE You have no business now with Jack that doesn't include me. If Jack goes, I go.

AUSTIN This includes you.

MRS. METHERELL Jack doesn't go. Jack stays where he is.

AUSTIN *(trying to be dignified)* Do you know who I am?

MRS. METHERELL You're the man who's flitting me to Birchester. Turning me out of my house, me that's lived in Blackton all my life, to go to a strange town and buy in strange shops where'll they rob me, and live beside strangers instead of here where everybody knew me for the mother of Jack Metherell.

ELSIE But from what Jack says, Mrs. Metherell, Blackton won't be very pleasant for you now.

MRS. METHERELL *(hotly)* Who's made it so?

AUSTIN Mrs. Metherell, can't we be friends? I've always been on friendly terms in Club affairs with Jack, until to-day.

MRS. METHERELL A lot can happen in a day.

AUSTIN Yes. To-day the club has died.

ELSIE Died!

AUSTIN Yes. You know something of what the club has meant to me. I made it, built it, fostered it, and now it's dead. There's been a meeting since the match. The other directors had pence in where I had pounds. They won't put another farthing down to save the club, and I can't. I'm ruined. But that isn't what I'm here for now. I've lost to-day a greater thing than money.

ELSIE Ruined! Father, what do you mean?

MRS. METHERELL You needn't fret. Ruined is a way of talking. He'll have a nest-egg left to pay your servants and your milliner's bills.

AUSTIN No. It means literally ruined. Metherell has cause to know my case was pretty desperate.

JACK I didn't know how bad.

AUSTIN Could you have acted any differently if you had?

JACK You know I couldn't.

AUSTIN (sincerely) No. You've showed up well to-day, and I've showed badly.

JACK (sympathetically) You were in a hole.

AUSTIN A man can never tell beforehand what he'll do in a tight corner, but he can be ashamed afterwards if he's done the wrong thing. And I'm—I'm trying now to snatch some rags of self-respect. Won't you help me, Mrs. Metherell?

MRS. METHERELL (graciously) Well, maybe a drowning man can't be particular what straw he clutches at. What can I do?

AUSTIN Jack was the straw I clutched. I tempted him, and, to his honour and my own dishonour, he withstood me. But I owe him reparation, and I want to pay. If I can see these two young people happy, I shan't feel utterly debased. I shall have rescued from the wreck enough to give me back my soul.

MRS. METHERELL (hardening again) That's a grand high way to talk about a bit of conscience-money.

AUSTIN (humbly) Yes, call it conscience-money if you like, although I have no money now, and money won't buy me back my peace of mind. I'm going to do the one thing in my power to right the wrong I did to Jack this afternoon. I'm going to put this marriage through.

MRS. METHERELL *(ironically)* Oh? What marriage may that be?

AUSTIN Don't you know?

ELSIE Of course she knows.

AUSTIN Then that's all right, and a load's gone off my mind.

ELSIE One moment, father.

AUSTIN Yes. What is it?

ELSIE I'm not so confident about it as I was.

AUSTIN As you were when? It's not an hour since you defied the world to stand between you and Jack.

ELSIE It's not the world that stands between. It's Mrs. Metherell.

JACK Elsie! *(Going towards her, then standing bewildered)*

AUSTIN Mrs. Metherell! *(Turning to her genially)* Oh, come, we parents have to make this sacrifice to see our children happy.

MRS. METHERELL I care as much about Jack's happiness as you.

AUSTIN Then we're unanimous. That's settled then.

ELSIE *(quietly)* Not quite.

AUSTIN Why not. *(Looking at JACK)* You told me my consent was all you wanted.

MRS. METHERELL *(eyeing JACK)* Did you?

JACK No. I said I'd want yours too.

AUSTIN Of course. Well, you've got my consent now, freely, gladly given.

JACK Yes, I wanted that.

AUSTIN Isn't that everything?

ELSIE No. I've been thinking.

AUSTIN I thought you knew your own mind, Elsie.

ELSIE I didn't know Mrs. Metherell. Perhaps I didn't know Jack.

AUSTIN *(still with confidence)* There's been some lovers' tiff between you. Come, Elsie, I divided you this afternoon. Let me unite you now. What is the difficulty? I'm sure it's just a temporary trifle.

ELSIE Whether it's temporary depends on how long Mrs. Metherell proposes to live.

MRS. METHERELL *(enjoying herself)* I'm hearty, thank you. Mine's a long-lived family.

AUSTIN *(brushing the difficulty aside)* Mrs. Metherell won't stand in your way, Elsie.

MRS. METHERELL Speak for yourself.

AUSTIN Oh, now I see. You're feeling as I did. It took me by surprise. But I'm converted now, and you'll find you'll soon grow used to the idea. Once you and I were young ourselves, and—

ELSIE Father, it's no use talking to Mrs. Metherell as if she was a reasonable being. It rests with Jack to choose.

JACK To choose?

ELSIE Yes. Me or your mother. Which is it to be?

JACK I—I don't know. *(Glancing shiftily at MRS. METHERELL)*

MRS. METHERELL *(menacingly)* You'd better know, and sharp.

JACK She's my mother, Elsie.

ELSIE Yes. Who comes first? Your mother or the woman you— the woman I used to think you loved.

JACK *(hurt)* Elsie, you know I love you.

ELSIE Do I? Is it love? Love hasn't widened your horizon. Love should break through, but you can't see beyond your mother for all your love.

AUSTIN *(peace-making)* Elsie, you mustn't ask a man to make a choice like that. These relationships don't clash. They sort themselves out.

ELSIE That's all you know about it. If you'd been here earlier, you'd have seen the clash all right.

AUSTIN I didn't see it, but I know you're very capable of looking after yourself.

ELSIE Oh, I can manage you. And I can manage

JACK You're men, but—

MRS. METHERELL You can't manage me.

ELSIE *(agreeing)* I've met my match.

AUSTIN *(earnestly)* Elsie, I've set my heart on seeing you happy. My future's black. I see no future for myself at all, but I hoped that this one satisfaction would be granted me. You wanted Jack.

ELSIE Yes, but—

AUSTIN Do you still want him?

ELSIE He's got a mother.

AUSTIN Never mind her. Do you want him?

ELSIE Yes. By himself.

AUSTIN Very well. Metherell, do you want her?

JACK My mother doesn't want me to want her.

AUSTIN No. But do you?

JACK It's like this—

ELSIE It's no good, father. If wishing could kill Mrs. Metherell, she'd be dead at my feet.

JACK Elsie!

MRS. METHERELL Plain speaking breaks no bones. I can give as good as I get.

AUSTIN May I speak plainly, then? Frankly, don't you think your attitude is selfish. We've all to see our children go from us, or the world would never get on. Let me appeal to you— and I think you will acknowledge that a man of my position is not accustomed to appeal to a woman of—well, you'll admit the difference between us, and the fact that I make very earnestly this petition should—

MRS. METHERELL Yes. I'll admit the difference between us. You're ruined. I'm not.

AUSTIN *(taken aback)* Ruined!

MRS. METHERELL Didn't you say so?

AUSTIN *(bitterly)* Yes. I'm ruined.

MRS. METHERELL You've a family. It's a good lift to a ruined man with a family to get a daughter off his hands. That's why you've come to push her on to us. We mayn't be swells, but we can keep her, and that's more than you can do, so—

AUSTIN *(to* JACK*)* Metherell, you don't believe that, do you ?

JACK *(avoiding* MRS. METHERELL'*s eye)* No. I think you're sorry you forgot yourself this morning.

AUSTIN I've done my best to make amends.

JACK Yes.

AUSTIN Is it—?

ELSIE Yes, father. It's impossible.

JACK Elsie!

ELSIE *(to* JACK*)* Isn't it impossible?

JACK *(after a pause while he looks from* ELSIE *to* MRS. METHERELL, *finally meeting* MRS. METHERELL'*s eye and bending his head)* Yes.

EDMUND *knocks and enters without waiting.*

EDMUND May I come in?

AUSTIN You here, Edmund!

EDMUND I came back for Elsie. I've been looking for you everywhere.

MRS. METHERELL Well, now you've found him, you'd better take him away. I'll be charging some of you rent for the use of my room.

EDMUND But what's happened?

ELSIE Oh, you've won.

EDMUND. I've won?

ELSIE Yes. The old guard. You and Mrs. Metherell.

MRS. METHERELL Yes. You saw it wouldn't do. You're the only Whitworth in your senses.

EDMUND Thank you, Mrs. Metherell.

AUSTIN *(cornering* **EDMUND**, *anxiously)* You know we lost the match.

EDMUND Yes. What are you going to do?

AUSTIN I've not had time to think about myself. This affair came first.

EDMUND Well, this is where I come in.

AUSTIN *(with a touch of an elder brothers contempt)* What can you do? The club's wound up.

EDMUND If I like, I can do a good deal. I'm a bachelor with a good city practice, and no expensive hobbies, Austin.

AUSTIN *(bitterly)* I never thought it would come to this. My young brother.

EDMUND Not so young. Oh, if it stings a bit, perhaps it ought to. You'd the old man's house and the lion's share of his money, and I've got to pull you out of the hole you dug yourself. There's only one person who'll like it less than you, and that's my energetic nephew.

AUSTIN Leo!

EDMUND I'll present Master Leo with his articles. The law's a splendid cure for lungs and laziness.

JACK *(approaching* **EDMUND***)* Mr. Whitworth, there's no ill feeling, is there ?

EDMUND Not a bit.

JACK And Mr. Austin fancies he owes me something.

EDMUND Oh?

AUSTIN I have that bribery business badly on my mind.

EDMUND What do you want, Metherell?

JACK I'm a man with ambitions, sir, and I heard what you said about Mr. Leo. Would you give me my articles?

EDMUND My friend, you're an excellent footballer, but you'd make a shocking lawyer with that delicate conscience of yours.

MRS. METHERELL You'll go on living honestly, Jack.

JACK (*submissively*) Yes, mother.

MRS. METHERELL And when you marry I'll choose you a decent hard-working girl who'll look after you properly, and not a butter-fingered lass who'll break your crockery and want waiting on hand and foot and —

EDMUND Mrs. Metherell!

MRS. METHERELL Oh, I forgot you were there. I was just talking privately to my son, same as you've been doing amongst yourselves.

EDMUND We've earned that. I beg your pardon, Mrs. Metherell.

ELSIE Good-bye, Jack.

JACK (*taking her hand*) Good-bye, Miss Whitworth.

ELSIE *turns her face away.* EDMUND *opens door.*

AUSTIN (*shaking his hand*) Metherell, I'm sorry.

JACK You did your best to make it right.

Exit AUSTIN.

EDMUND (*at door*) Elsie.

ELSIE (*going to him*) Yes, uncle?

EDMUND (*going out with his arm round her*) London!

ELSIE *smiles gladly at him as they go out* MRS. METHERELL *places teapot on table.* JACK *sits and resumes his tea.*

Curtain

Note

*—The "transfer" of a football player from one team to another
cannot now be made with the rapidity shown in this play. At the
time when "The Game" was written, such a transfer was possible.
A year or two earlier, indeed transfers were made at least as quickly
as in the play—and one is allowed a certain licence of compression
in a play. The instance in point is recorded in the "Worlds Work"
for September, 1912, In an article entitled, "Is Football a Business?"
Mr. J. J. Bentley, ex-president and life member of the Football League,
tells how he effected the transfer of a player named Charles Roberts
from Grimsby to Manchester United on a Friday night, the player
being at Grimsby, and Mr. Bentley in London. The matter was
settled by telephone at midnight, and in sixteen hours after signing
Roberts appeared in the Manchester United Colours.*